Phenomenal Pets
A Collection of
Mystical Tales

Phenomenal Pets
A Collection of
Mystical Tales

Saraina Hancock, MA

iUniverse, Inc.
New York Lincoln Shanghai

Phenomenal Pets A Collection of Mystical Tales

iUniverse books may be ordered through booksellers or by contacting:

iUniverse
2021 Pine Lake Road, Suite 100
Lincoln, NE 68512
www.iuniverse.com
1-800-Authors (1-800-288-4677)

Because of the dynamic nature of the Internet, any Web addresses
or links contained in this book may have changed
since publication and may no longer be valid.

ISBN: 978-0-595-44261-4 (pbk)
ISBN: 978-0-595-88591-6 (ebk)

Printed in the United States of America

Manuscript Editor: Jeri Helen
Editorial Associate: Jeannette Dames
Mentor: Helen Weber
Cover Design: Saraina Hancock and Chris Litchfield
Photography: Saraina Hancock
Photographs: Zebulon by Julie Horne
Photographs: Tasha Rose by Jai Tomlin
Photographs: Samantha by Brian Stone

Contents

PART II   PET-POURRI: A COLLECTION OF SHORT TALES

Acknowledgements

Dedicated to my incredible family, who taught me
that love transcends time and space, even language

The Hancock Family
Beth, Gramma Tina, Marvin, Saraina, Torii and Mary

Special thanks to the generous people
who shared their wonderful stories of beloved pets

Blessings and appreciation to our animal companions
for their indelible spirits, loyalty and love

Gratitude to my mentor Helen, editors Jeri and Jeanette
and graphic designer Chris

Preface

o o o o o o o o o o o o o o o o o o o o o o o o o o o o

*One day science will understand what faith has known
all along*

—*Ashleigh Brilliant*

The focus of my life's work for the past twenty years has been
the reclamation of our essential nature: digging for the buried
treasure within. My educational journey has led me to concur
with the philosophy that we were once deeply connected with
the Earth and all of nature. From this place, all beings communicated through unspoken language, were one with Source, and
contributed their actions to the benefit of all. Each aspect of cre-
ation was held in reverence and respect; the plants, animals and
minerals were valued participants in the passionate play unfolding around us. We did not separate ourselves from the natural
world until the introduction of written language[1], at which time
our innate perceptual process gave way to abstract thinking;
then we severed ourselves from the delicate web of "right rela-
tions" and lost our perspective of universal unity.

Our animal brothers and sisters still live within the dynamic
union of oneness. This is why they model the best qualities on
Earth: unconditional love, selfless service, and loyalty. They live
in the present, they communicate with each other and with

those who are open to understanding them, and their presence as companions offers us profound mental, physical and spiritual benefits.

My hope is that through the true stories written here, we may catch a glimpse of the incredible potential of our animal partners, and be inspired to tap deeper into our own intuitive resources.

Got Tales?

If there's one thing I learned while collecting these incredible stories, it's that everyone has them! I deeply enjoyed sharing the adventures and experiences of the pets and people in this book and I plan to continue this work with the following intentions:

- Tithe back to the animals—too many are left abandoned and homeless; they need our unconditional support!

- Increase awareness of the inherent benefits of pet ownership: mental, emotional, physical and spiritual.

- Decrease the number of pets who are neglected by educating the public and networking.

- Honor the unsung heroes and "sheroes" of our lives—they deserve it!

- Create a forum where folks can share stories, news, resources and ideas about their beloved animals.

If you have stories, pictures, news or information you'd love to share, you can do so online: www.phenomenalpets.com

Also, if you know of a nonprofit or charity that does exceptional work for the animals, please tell me. I'll do my best to spread the word and offer support!

Warmest regards, Saraina and Lylin

PART I
Dog Tales

Weasel the Wonder Dog

My Greatest Teacher

o o o o o o o o o o o o o o o o o o o o o o o o o o o

Live your life as though every act were to become a universal law.

—*Henry David Thoreau*

Autumn ... I love returning to school, learning, meeting people, the sun's perfect temperature as trees surrender their leaves in a glorious, golden salute! Basking on the porch, a warm breeze tossed my hair and caressed my face while music wafted from our funky duplex.

Studying sociology at Washington State University, life glided with ease and simplicity—a plentitude of friends and activities happening around the clock. My academic process was secondary to the real-life education unfurling; classes were a backdrop for my blooming social life and personal evolution. However, my greatest teacher was about to arrive.

Early in the semester, Kris, a friend of a friend, appeared at my door with a scruffy, orange Maltese-Terrier. She and the 8-pound pup stood expectantly on my doorstep while she relayed her tale of how the wee woof found his way into the Burger King where she worked. "He was cowering under a table, hungry and frightened." Kris, being the kindest of souls, fed him

3

and placed him gently in her car. She took him home, intent on searching for his owner, but she lived in an apartment where the manager threatened to throw her out and keep her deposit unless the dog went. Her plea to me (since my landlord allowed pets) was to keep him until we found his owner or a suitable home.

I stood at the door, in shock over the suddenness of her request—*me,* take a dog—NOW? I was reluctant since I was at school all day and being newly in love, out late every night. Uncomfortably, I assessed the despondent pooch: his fur was dirty and matted, cut short in an unpleasing style, and one of his ears stuck out as though it was injured or deformed. From his bedraggled looks, it was clear he'd been on the road for a while, run-away or abandoned. Without too much hesitation, I agreed to take him in.

Diligently, we posted signs around town, but no one stepped forward to claim the missing pooch. Initially, I agreed to keep him for a week, then we'd decide what to do next. A week came and went with no word from his previous home; now his fate was up to me. When it came right down to it, I couldn't turn my back on this precious soul. Despite his dowdy looks, there was something special about him—he was a "diamond in the rough".

Fondly, we named him "Weasel the Wonder Dog" mostly because he actually resembled a weasel with his bad haircut. He was also timid, running behind the couch any time someone new came in. He cowered and shook if you looked sideways at him; it was sadly apparent that his life to this point had not been plush or even pleasant.

However, his luck had changed; with a bath and a new keeper, things were looking up. Straight away I let his fur grow out, except around his eyes so he had a clear view. I treated him kindly and even let him sleep on my bed, but I was still gone a lot and discovered this did not work! I would come home to a little "present" in the middle of the floor; he was fully house-trained and highly intelligent—it was a commentary, not an accident, and his point was clear.

Since I couldn't slow my life down, I decided he'd have to come with me, and so he did, everywhere I went. These were simpler times; in a small town, it was easy to include him on my journey. We went to class; if it was sunny, he waited outside in the shade with snacks, water and other dogs. If it was cold, he rode inside my parka—his furry face peeking over the zipper, generating grins from passersby. Everywhere we went, people fell in love with this little guy. His sweet, unassuming spirit was irresistible.

My affinity for dogs was apparent from early childhood. Penned lovingly in my baby book under "likes" at age 3 are the words, "loves music and any dog".

More telling is the entry under "gifts received" for my 4th birthday: "A card and 50 cents from Woodsy the dog". In our family, dogs were cherished—not only were they invited to the party, they even brought gifts!

Although I loved dogs, I'd never had my very own. Weasel granted me the honor of witnessing the profound, healing power of love. Once his outer reality shifted, his inner world followed, transforming him into an adorable four-legged fluff ball; even his crooked ear mended.

The Profound Healing Power of Love

His appearance shifted so dramatically from the original lost dog that when Kris stopped by six months later, she didn't recognize him. In a concerned tone, she asked, "What happened to the dog I left with you—why did you get another one?" I laughed gleefully, "Kris, it's the same dog!" She seriously did not believe me, even as he came running up to greet her—when it finally did sink in, she was utterly blown away.

Before our eyes stood living proof—love is a catalyst for pure magic. Weasel had become a "joy generator". His playful spirit and incredibly cute exterior ignited smiles instantly. I began to notice how the mood picked up around him; while folks stroked his fur and massaged his ears, those nearby enjoyed the overflow of love. The benefits were immediate and concrete, and there is now scientific evidence that any act of kindness experienced or observed boosts serotonin levels, elevating one's mood and strengthening the immune systems of all present.[2]

His confidence was soaring; he pranced beside me, head high, tail straight up. Such a personality was he, folks around town began to call him *"The Wease"*—he became a little celebrity, complete with a circle of pals who knew him wherever he went.

His zest for living life to the fullest was contagious. At parties he would sidle up to the drip tray beneath the keg and sip some beer like everyone else, although he preferred cocktails left unattended by their owners. I didn't encourage this behavior, but he was quick, clever and cute; you had to keep an eye on him. With a little libation in his belly he would flirt around the room, successfully commandeering treats from adoring females. Then he'd return like a pirate with booty so I could confiscate anything he shouldn't eat.

Weasel had a kitty-cat pal in our communal house, of the same size and color, who bore the outlandish name Schmedlick. They were a smart match and loved to show off at gatherings. They'd spar in the middle of the room, inducing guests to cheer as they pummeled each other like TV wrestlers. After the show, you'd find them basking in adoration, collecting strokes and snacks from fans. These enterprising companions collaborated on their act; they never engaged aggressively without an audience.

As seasons changed, the closeness of our connection deepened. I too was undergoing a transition: my heart opened and I began to evolve in ways I did not anticipate. "The Wease" modeled the art of giving and receiving so graciously with everyone he touched. The effects cascaded through my own life, deepening the quality of relationships with my family, friends and partner. I observed that the more love I gave, the more I was able to experience. The Law of Attraction dictates that whatever you focus on expands[3]—I've found this to be profoundly true.

Furthermore, my romance with physics and parapsychology led me deeper into the canine psyche. I began to understand that animals are "energy readers"—they perceive thoughts and feelings (not just words and actions), then respond accordingly. This means that if you expect great things from your pet, great things you will get; if you regard them as inferior or unintelligent, well they can emulate that too—they're built to please, after all.

Through my understanding of emerging research in quantum mechanics and through direct observation, I began to believe that much of what we call "extra-sensory" perception is *standard* for animals.

They appear to possess the natural ability to take in the subtle streams of consciousness that we completely ignore because they are living in "the field" without the filters of verbal language. This field, known as "zero point," binds our world seamlessly in "an ocean of microscopic vibrations in the space between things.... a heaving sea of energy—one vast quantum field".[4]

Apollo astronaut Ed Mitchell felt the presence of this invisible web as he floated above the Earth; he glimpsed the oneness of the universe and experienced transcendence of time and language. "There seemed to be an enormous force field connecting all people, their intentions and thoughts and every animate and inanimate form of matter for all time ... Linear time was an artificial construct."[5]

Incredible as it sounds, we don't need to leave the Earth to find "the field"—it's fully available right where we are.

I witnessed evidence of this uncanny ability every night at dinner. Our sweet terrier would be sleeping in his bed oblivious of my actions. However, the moment a thought entered my mind to put food scraps in his bowl, he would sit up and wag his tail. He was not getting any physical, visual or verbal clues from me; he was sensing a thought the moment it formed in my mind.

Fritjof Capra presents historical evidence suggesting that prelanguage humans had greater perceptual abilities:

As the diversity and richness of our human relationships increased, our humanity—our language, art, thought, and culture—unfolded accordingly. At the same time, we also developed the ability of abstract thinking, of bringing forth an inner world of concepts, objects and images of ourselves. Gradually, as this inner world became ever more diverse and complex, we began to lose touch with nature and became ever more fragmented personalities.[6]

Although our intuitive awareness may be submerged, we can regain it if we so desire. Once I understood Weasel's telepathic ability, I wanted to understand and utilize my own; gradually we began to send thoughts between us in a continuous fashion. I knew this is was not unusual for those who are close. My parents shared telepathic experiences when my father was in the Korean War.

When I was four, Mother had woken with a start, fearing something happened to my father. A few anxious days passed, then a letter arrived confirming her experience: a flash flood hit the area where he was stationed. As he was running across a wooden foot-bridge, raging waters swept him off his feet and over the edge. In desperation, he grabbed the side of the bridge as he lost his footing. A miraculous combination of timing and movement allowed his wedding ring to catch a protruding nail, saving him. Except for a sprained finger, our father was safe.

My parents showed us how true love transcends time and space, even language. So it felt quite natural to have this connection with my four-legged best friend.

When my "little buddy" wanted my attention, I would receive an insight and "tune in" to him. One such time, we were picnicking down at Snake River; it seemed the entire campus came to bask in the sun glinting through the canyon. Gazing lazily at the sky, I became aware of Weasel asking for my interest, so I pulled my focus from the blue canopy to see where he'd gone. I sensed no danger, just a "look at me, look at me" message. I scanned the horizon to find him running like the wind, with a line of dogs chasing behind him. There were big dogs, little dogs, old and young dogs; Weasel was leading the parade, dodging picnickers, blankets and umbrellas, racing up and down the bank till everyone on the river was following his adventure. No dog could catch him; he was lightening-fast and super agile. Still, they mirrored every movement to stay in line. On-lookers began cheering as he raced by; ears streaming in the wind, he kicked it into high gear for one more sweep around the canyon then ended the caravan at our blanket. Panting in jubilation, dogs scattered back to their respective owners.

In those moments, we shared the thrill of being fully present and alive!

Our forty-acre farm near Duvall, Washington

Weasel exploring the farm

Adventures on the Farm

After graduation, my partner Michael and I migrated west, settling on a forty-acre farm near Duvall, Washington. Weasel relished wide-open fields where he'd run with horses, cows, chickens and pigs. The farm was a living cornucopia: several varieties of apples, plums, pears and grapes flourished there.

One day, working intently in my garden, I had the distinct impression Weasel was in danger. The feeling swept over me like a wave of adrenaline. Poised on the edge of the energy, I began sourcing it out and heard what I already knew: Weasel was in BIG trouble. From the pig-pen came frightened cries and yelps. Somehow he'd slipped in under the electric wire and was now running in blind panic, coated in thick mud as giant hogs tried to trample him. I sprang to a full sprint, leapt into the pen and grabbed him by the scruff of the neck, then took the terrified terrier inside to check for injuries.

After a bath, we calmed down and realized how narrow the margin was for a safe rescue. Holding him as he rested, I thanked heavens above for our unconventional communication: a telepathic tie that saved his life.

Michael's best friend, also named Michael, moved in with us. Traveling six months of the year, communal living gave him a happy place to land between trips. The house itself was modest yet roomy, with a well-worn rough wood interior. The kitchen had parquet floors, a pantry and sun room adorned with sweeping views of the Cascade Mountains and Snoqualmie River. It felt like home!

Our farm was a perfect gathering place for families and friends; there was food and room for all. Weasel loved people, with one exception: a guest who'd set him off. He'd bark when he arrived, bark every time he saw the guy ... he did NOT approve. I rather agreed, but he was married to a dear friend so we welcomed him. Still, I wondered what message Weasel was relaying; his behavior was not random.

In *Kinship with All Life*, Boone tells of Strongheart, a highly intelligent Shepard who sensed dishonesty. This justice-seeking canine cornered folks with ill intentions or criminal records.[7] We soon learned that Weasel had the same good sense; the man was having an affair, and I believe Weasel barked at the injustice of it. From that point forward, I paid greater attention to Weasel's response to people who entered our happy home.

With each season came adventure: springtime meant rising rivers. One morning after we left for work, the valley flooded and we couldn't get home. Our house was safe—it sat on high ground—but the surrounding roads were submerged. I panicked when I realized Weasel was cut off. Should we buy a boat and paddle home? What could we do? From the hill above we saw lights at the dairy farm; our neighbors Randy and Linda stayed for their cattle, and they kindly promised to care for my little woof.

We stayed with our dear friend Jana, but every minute away was hard. I would check in with him each night as I drifted to sleep, connecting heart to heart, sending love and hoping to be home soon.

By the third day, water on the main roads receded. We drove out hoping to make it to the farm. The property was still covered in mirror-calm water, which welcomed us deceptively. Below the surface—DANGER—you can't know the edge of the road, the depth factor or what objects lurk beneath.

We stood at the end of our driveway, sinking with the thought of driving back to town. I couldn't bear leaving Weasel alone any longer. Suddenly, our neighbor Randy swung around the bend on his combine. He spied our silhouettes in the twilight, and then drove to the edge of the water. "Hey over there!" he shouted. We yelled back, "When's this crazy flood due to end?"

Bantering back and forth, we were making light of our unpleasant situation, but he could tell our spirits were wilted. With barely a word, he trolled into the water, feeling his way along our quarter-mile driveway in his quarter-million-dollar machine. We were stunned by his compassion and held our breath as he moved cautiously through murky water in fading light.

The moon crested the horizon, its disc-like presence made the scene surreal … stars twinkled, it felt late. What if Randy ended up in the ditch because of us? On pins and needles, we watched—inch by inch, he made his way to our rescue. Cheering, we scrambled up on the huge mechanical ark.

Now to get back! It was darker yet, and we slipped into pitch-black water—edgeless, endless. Our captain was guided by pure intuition and we were riding on it. Four people holding their breath is ominous, like deep sea divers drawing only that needed to survive. Quietly, quietly, closer, closer … then, wheels on dry land and a giant exhale—he did it! How did he stay on the road, blinded by water and darkness?

Gratitude is too small a word for his act of selfless kindness—risking so much for a neighbor. Our hearts overflowed with love—*we were home!* Thanking him and running simultaneously, I scrambled for keys to open the door … LET ME IN!!

Weasel leapt into my arms; he was shaken but safe. Everything was instantly better! After a warm bath and tea, we crawled into our waterbed—ah, water where it should be! We slept soundly without a care.

Upon our return we discovered the farm served as refuge for a tribe of mice—harmless grey visitors, yet too many to ignore. As I chopped veggies for dinner, one strolled over my foot. "MOUSE!" I shrieked instinctively and sprinted up the stairs. Michael and Michael raced to my rescue; Weasel barked ATTACK! Armed with Tupperware, they charged the mini-invader, quickly corralling him. But then, to everyone's surprise he charged back—the "M's" scattered, leaving Weasel whisker to whisker with his petite opponent. Fearlessly it reared up and charged again, startling The Wease so much his feet skittered in all directions to get away.

From the safety of the staircase, I laughed till my cheeks hurt—two grown men and a "vicious" canine toppled by a 2-inch rodent with *attitude*! Never underestimate the power of intention, even in the face of daunting odds.

The valley dried, spring rolled into summer, there was wonderful work to be done: weeding, watering, harvesting and chopping wood. I followed some advice I found in *The Garden Primer* and planted extra rows for the critters. The idea is that after setting aside a generous share for the natural residents, you may communicate with them and request that your sets be spared. Thus, as cultivators of the Earth, we can align with the natural partnership between all living things in a spirit of generosity and become participants in the circle of life.[8]

I would never use toxic pesticides on the land or our food, so I went with the author's philosophy. Amazing as it sounds, it worked splendidly; our tomatoes were perfect—huge, brilliant red orbs—untouched row after row (and the critters were fed).

As days lengthened, Weasel and I created a fabulous routine: we worked intensely through the brisk morning, then meditated and relaxed on the deck as heat rose in the valley. At noon I opened the French doors to our deck; music spilled into the fresh air summoning cattle to gather along the fence. They joined us each day at lunchtime, watching silently, munching for hours.

A few weeks into our ritual, the cattle would literally race across the fields at noon—for the music, the company? Whatever their motivation, I greeted them with a warm wave and smile. In our world, we had plenty of love to share!

Another noontime attraction was our neighbor's youngest son, Jerry, who loved to play show-and-tell with us "city farmers". He brought us baby chicks, kittens and tiny mice. It was wonderful until he brought a snake in a shoe box; this evoked a pretty large shriek, ending his infatuation with "non-country folks".

We hadn't seen him for weeks, when a worried Linda came
to the door asking if he'd been over. "No, not since the snake
adventure," I reported. He'd been missing for over an hour, and
by the concerned look in her eyes I knew this was irregular.
There are many places a boy can go on a farm, including dangerous places, like the manure pit or river; there are wild animals too. Still, this kid was savvy—he knew his way around.
Where could he have disappeared to for so long?

I turned to Weasel: can you find him? His ears perked with a
definitive "YES"! We sat for a moment; I tuned into the impressions he was sending and got the word "*sleeping*". He was taking
a nap ... but where? We scrambled out the door to test our theory, and Randy was already waving to us with news: the lad was
found napping in a nearby field. Rubbing his eyes in his
mother's arms, he looked puzzled about the fuss.

Summer acquiesced to fall. We canned, froze and stored a
bountiful harvest from our garden, enjoyed home-grown pump-
kins, hayrides and haunted houses. One late-autumn evening,
Weasel and I sat on the deck watching a double rainbow over
the valley. The weather was changing—you could feel it.

The two Michaels were on their way home from the grocery
store. Light fading, we sauntered inside, but the room felt
strange—something was wrong! Weasel ran to the lamp barking. I heard buzzing, louder, louder.... straining to see as I
backed out of the room, several flew at me—FLIES! Pools of
light from every lamp were blackened with hundreds of flies.
Run! Mice I could handle, but a fly invasion was overwhelming—even for someone who appreciates all forms of life!

We raced back onto the porch, skin crawling from the experience; there was no way to call the guys for help ... we simply

had to wait. Darkness encroached. I was cold but didn't want to go back into "fly horror" to get a sweater. An hour passed like a day; huddled together on the deck, we saw headlights on the drive.

The M's pulled in and we ran toward them shouting broken phrases: "FLIES—taken over the house; it's a nightmare, what are we going to do …?" Sure, we sounded utterly mad, but it didn't take long to prove our point. Somehow, swarms of flies had wriggled their way through the wooden walls as the sun went down, drawn to warm pools of light inside.

Why it happened, we never knew, but our neighbors reported the previous renters had a similar experience. It was time to move!

Island in the City

o o o o o o o o o o o o o o o o o o o o o o o o o o o o o

Reality is merely an illusion, albeit a very persistent one

—Albert Einstein

Back in the city, we enjoyed shops and restaurants with sweeping views from Queen Anne Hill. Our new home was bright and airy with a splendid split-level deck; a stand of birch trees graced our windows with green leaves and song birds. On our nightly walks, we drank in brilliant sunsets over Elliot Bay—a neighborhood ritual shared by all.

Working downtown as a systems analyst, I rarely had to work overtime, but things began to pile up, so I brought home a terminal and modem so I could meet approaching deadlines. Weasel watched me type into the strange box from the couch with distain, sighing loudly to let me know I wasn't doing my part to entertain him. I suggested he should be thankful I could work from home rather than the office, in which case he'd have no company at all.

I arrived the following evening to find the modem cable severed with the precision of a surgeon. Somehow, he knew exactly which connection rendered "the box" useless. He didn't damage any other cables and fortunately didn't bite the power cord, but he halted my operation with a single chomp!

It slowed my progress; it didn't change the deadlines. In a panic, I sought assistance from our neighbor who kindly spliced the wire back together. He too was mystified and impressed that Weasel sabotaged the modem with such ease. How could he have known—terrier intuition?

Before long, I was back to work; Weasel seemed satisfied that we acknowledged his caper even if it didn't completely halt my process.

As the crimson sun began its descent, I finished entering data, and off we went for a long, refreshing walk under the evening colors.

Our next great adventure was a lingerie party on the upper deck; all my lady friends attended, including my mom and my (female) boss—it was big fun!

It started with a fashion show and a game called "most sensuous"—we filled out a questionnaire with points for answers such as "When's the last time you had a candlelight dinner or soaked in a hot tub?" Everyone added their points—my *mom* won by a landslide! She and father were amazingly in love after 50 years of marriage!

Weasel was bestowed the honor of wearing her prize in lieu of his normal collar—a purple garter that read "Most Sensuous" on it. In the morning (still wearing the garter), he wandered down to the yard as he did everyday. But this particular day he became disoriented and lost in minutes. I was freaking out, searching everywhere! Posters went up all over the hill: a photo of The Wease with the description "Wearing purple garter with

'Most Sensuous' on it". This must have helped identify him quickly and he was rescued several frantic hours later.

Weasel was now fifteen and beginning to age. He went out his dog-door in the middle of the night, but, due to his failing night vision, he became paralyzed at the top of a steep set of stairs leading to the backyard. Confused and frightened, he was about to fall.

With a jolt, I awoke from a deep sleep and raced out to the deck to find him teetering dangerously on the top step. His cry was so soft it was unperceivable except by my "psychic ears". Once again, our telepathy saved his life that night.

True Nectar

o o o o o o o o o o o o o o o o o o o o o o o o o o

Let the beauty you love be what you do

—Rumi

For most of Weasel's life I worked as a systems administrator, then after 12 years I grew restless. I was drawn to an old enchantment which began in the fifth grade. While our class-mates enjoyed *Mrs. Piggle-Wiggle* and *Pippy Longstocking*, my best friend Kari and I discovered Hans Holzer, Ghost Hunter and the renowned English transmedium Sybil Leek. We shared a fascination with the mystery of hidden realties; it seemed we alone understood the intrigue.

In retrospect, I have immense appreciation for friendships built on such magical ground. Someone who listens wide-eyed, ready to jump into the adventure with both feet—what a mag-nificent, irreplaceable gift: a friend who believes.

John F. Kennedy encouraged us: "We have nothing to fear but, fear itself" and believing such, I never limited my mind, imagination or intuition. I began to ponder my passion out loud with my close friend Karen, who immediately connected with my interest. She narrated an exhilarating story about her mother who developed intuitive powers after being left on her own with four young daughters.

Her family owned a quaint lodge with 12 rustic cabins around a private lake. Ruthie, an elegant woman in her forties, greeted her guests by clasping their hands in hers, sensing their intentions before allowing them to stay. This was a priceless gift of perception born out of necessity—ensuring the safety of her children.

After her children were grown, she retired and remained at the lake lodge using her well-developed intuitive skills to share insights with clients who pulled up in Mercedes Benz and BMWs—her subsidy to social security!

I was mesmerized by her tale of courage and brilliance and wanted to meet her right away! Luckily, Ruthie had a visit planned—I had the honor of meeting her and experiencing her abilities first-hand.

Ruthie was a striking woman; her long silvery hair was fashioned in braids and pinned up in spirals on each side. Most notably, she communicated with every form of life around her! "The plant on the window requests water," she announced casually. Later, she reported, "The dog is moving due to the pain in his hip; he hopes it will stay behind on the floor and not follow him".

Gentle and gracious, there was nothing boastful about her—she simply stated her observations in a relaxed matter-of-fact manner.

I respectfully requested a reading from her, to which she replied, "Oh yes, my dear, I am completely at your service". The generosity of this phrase remains with me today—I always begin my sessions with a question: "How may I be of service?"

We settled in at the kitchen table. Ruthie performed a "fin-ger-tip reading" by entwining our fingers and pressing our thumbs together. Stilling her mind, she shared her impressions; I was a hummingbird flitting flower to flower gathering nectar as I passed, but never stopping or standing still. Her advice: pick one "flower" that means the most to me and settle down with it. I listened!

Shortly after my encounter with Ruthie, I discovered a school for intuitive arts: The Psychic Institute's Clairvoyant Program. As Ruthie advised, I focused on what mattered most and moved into the most fabulous, exhilarating time of my life.

My reality was now an intriguing dichotomy: by day, I man-aged computer systems and by night I explored the depths of the psyche. At first, the contrast seemed stark; the left-brain world of machines adjacent to the right-brain realm of the mys-tical. Yet, as my awareness grew, I found there was no contrast, just a seamless web of interrelatedness between all things.

For example, now when a system crashed, instead of grab-bing a manual and troubleshooting "top-down", I found a quiet spot, focused my inner awareness, asked for an answer and found it was always there. Life became much easier!

The Final Years

∘ ∘

We are kept out of the Garden by our own fear

—Joseph Campbell

Weasel was now seventeen; I loved that little guy with every cell in my body. A fellow student at the Institute, Cory, was our groomer and pet intuitive. She came to the house for a monthly wash and check-in. Weasel and I communicated very well and yet, death was a difficult subject to broach. I thought it might be easier for both of us if she acted as "go between".

One evening after Cory finished washing and grooming Weasel, I asked her to check in and see how he was doing; specifically, I asked if he wanted to stay or go at this time in his life.

Cory knew how much we loved each other; she looked as us with deep compassion as she began "tuning in" to Weasel. My little buddy was rather fragile at this point. His tiny tail so thin, it just hung limply behind him; it didn't even wag. However, as Cory spoke on his behalf, his tail *did* wag enthusiastically each time she said something correct. I was amazed and grateful to learn this was possible. I asked Weasel if he was in pain. Cory said, "No, just tired." His tail wagged in agreement. I asked if he needed to go to the other side now? She said, "He was waiting to arrange another lifetime with me before he left". I was stunned … he can do that? "Oh yes," she explained. "Spirit is eternal, *all Spirit*, not just that of humans. He loves you and is worried about leaving you; he wants to be sure he can come back soon before he goes."

Again, his tail wagged deliberately, confirming the accuracy of her words. I mused, "This is fantastic, but how will I find him?"

"Don't worry," smiled Cory, "He'll find you."

On Christmas Eve, Weasel passed over. His absence was deeply felt, but I believed in my heart of hearts he would return, so I kept the faith and waited.

"As in the systems view, birth and death are seen by many traditions as stages of endless cycles which represent the continual self-renewal that is characteristic of the dance of life."
Fritjof Capra, The Turning Point [9]

Gretta Arrives!

Gretta's Silver Spirit

o o o o o o o o o o o o o o o o o o o o o o o o o o o o o

It is the secret of the world that all things subsist and do not die—They only retire a little from sight and afterward return again.

—*Ralph Waldo Emerson*

After Weasel's passing, I spent a good deal of time looking at dog books, trying to imagine what "he" might be next. My partner had a magnificent male Weimaraner named Gunnar. We thought a female of the same breed would be awesome; still, I felt I should just wait and see what happened.

So, wait I did. Then seven months to the day after Weasel's passing, the phone rang. I answered to find a breeder of Weimaraners on the line who "heard" I was looking for a puppy, no explanation of how or where. I didn't bother to ask.

She informed me she had a female puppy who needed a home; the proverbial light went on in my head—it's The Wease! Without hesitation, I said, "Yes, yes, when can we see her?" "Well," she said, "You can come right away, but you have to be interviewed, and I'm interviewing several couples". This was news to me; being interviewed to own a pet, what if I wasn't found fit to be a "dog mom" in her mind ... how would I ever get over that? Nervously, we hopped in the car heading for her kennel near Olympia.

On the way down, the synchronicity of the situation set in. People who know about Weimaraners know that breeders don't call you! In fact, waiting lists exist in Washington; folks have puppies flown in from other states "sight unseen". I was totally tickled by my unbelievably good fortune and in those moments of reckoning, I began to sense Weasel's presence. I can't say how, I simply knew—it was him. His spirit assured me everything would be alright and added that "she" wanted the name "Gretta" with two "t"s.

I pulled myself together as we arrived, then jumped out and hurried to the door in anticipation. After being greeted and seated, Diane, the owner of the kennel, brought forth the adorable grey baby. She was sweet and demure; I fell in love instantly. Diane watchfully set the tiny pup on the floor by my feet; with the skill of a gymnast, she clambered up my pant leg, licked my hand and fell asleep on my lap with a sigh. I wrapped my arms around her—we bonded blissfully.

Suddenly, momma dog rushed in and Diane commanded me, "Put her down, she might snap!" Before I could move a muscle, the mother was upon me. She raced up point blank, looked me straight in the eyes with a stare as stern as a police chief. Mama sniffed the puppy, checking for distress, then, pausing briefly, she removed her gaze and in an uncharacteristically calm manner, ambled out of the room. Diane looked puzzled, yet relieved, "Well, I guess she approves of you two."

Gretta and Gunnar getting acquainted

Traveling with Gretta and Gunnar

And so it was, Gretta joined our happy family. Purebreds are required to have a kennel name for their registration; her mother was "The Grey Ghost" and Gretta was named "The Silver Spirit".

Gunnar was five when Gretta joined us; their connection was strong and loyal. They shared a luxurious heated kennel with a double dog house. I remember the joy of seeing them side by side, heads popping out of their own little doors.

Living north of Seattle and working as a successful network administrator, we had an amazing life: traveling in our motor home, waterskiing off our boat. The two dogs ran, swam and romped gleefully in our two-acre yard. I felt deeply grateful and fortunate to be able to provide such a wonderful life for her.

Physically, Gretta was precious. Her silvery fur sparkled, and she had a white arrow with a half moon on her chest—very auspicious! Joy radiated from her angelic face; even grumpy people softened as they looked at her.

Psychically, she was an expert mind-reader from the start. I had to watch my thoughts. If I saw an adorable man, for example, Gretta would prance right up and nip his buns—imagine his surprise and mine! It was a great way to strike up a conversation and luckily most found it strangely amusing (including my partner).

I continued my research, sending and receiving thoughts with Gretta. She was super cooperative and highly intelligent; if we sent her a clear picture of what we wanted her to do, she'd "read us" then proceed to do it.

At the park one evening after we'd both endured long days, we were too tired for a lengthy walk. We decided to drive to a scenic overview of the bay for some fresh air. My partner noticed a gigantic boulder in the center of the park and mused out loud, "Do you think Gretta would run around it if I stood on top and held her leash?" I agreed that it would be a great way for her to run for a while—the distance around the rock was great enough to offer her some fun exercise without getting dizzy. We decided to send her "the picture" and see what happened.

I stayed below while he scrambled to the top of the massive stone, then I tossed up her lead; she looked confused until we both sent her a mental image of her running around the base of the boulder having fun and getting some well-needed exercise.

Immediately, she began trotting around the rock, slowly at first, then prancing with glee while we excitedly clapped for her. The people in the park thought we were nutty, but this never stopped us.

Our house-sitter noticed Gretta's mind-reading abilities the first night as she tucked herself in bed. Gretta appeared in the room with a questioning look, "May I come up?" Jen thought about it and decided it would be alright. Reportedly, Gretta waited until the exact moment the decision was made, then leapt up and snuggled down with no verbal command.

In the background of our happy life I was undergoing a major career change. I graduated from the Psychic Institute, began my private practice and quickly grew weary of my day job. It was crystal clear that working as a spiritual mentor was my true life's work, yet to counsel professionally I needed a master's degree in psychology. This seemed a rather lofty goal since I didn't even possess a bachelor's degree.

Still I persisted ... working both jobs, hoping for an opening to occur and visualizing what it might look like. Before long, an opening did occur; the company I worked for was purchased by a large Texas-based corporation that moved the entire operation to Texas where (they felt) labor and land were more affordable.

This magical turn of fate provided me with a generous severance package and the opportunity to return to school. I was *beyond* ecstatic and immediately launched my search for the appropriate college. Antioch University spoke my language and supported my vision!

Parents: Marvin and Beth were "Cool Cats"!

They deeply loved one another (and the beach) for 56 years.

Rebirth

Beyond our ideas of right-doing and wrong-doing, there is a field. I'll meet you there.
When the soul lies down in that grass, the world is too full to talk about.
Ideas, language, even the phrase 'each other' doesn't make sense any more

—Rumi

My world was spinning with a joyful hum. At last, a path I could passionately embrace. The tiny pieces of my journey wove themselves into a colorful, cohesive quilt. I felt the presence of a master plan.

Gretta and Gunnar were healthy and happy; we took trips in our motor home on the weekends to offset long workdays during the week. I was working for a mental health facility by day and attending Antioch University at night, the perfect balance of theory and practice—I was in heaven!

Then, like a tsunami, unexpected events shifted the calm with no warning. My beloved mother Beth had a series of mini strokes, which put her in a highly confused state. When I arrived at her house, her blood pressure was still at stroke level so I called 911 and we were off to the hospital.

Father and I waited patiently in the room, praying for the best. Finally, we heard voices in the hall, and I felt the presence of a kindred soul. "Kindred" meaning of the same tribe or clan, someone you know on sight—there are no words to describe it. You've probably felt it yourself or perhaps you've seen *The Highlander*; my experience relates to the sense an "immortal" gets when "one of their kind" comes within a certain distance—they feel them before they see them.

It was unexpected and uncanny, yet unmistakably real. My intuitive abilities were well developed at this time, but I'd never experienced anything this distinct: both doctors were moving toward me asking questions. My connection was with the younger of the two. Images were flooding my mind; I was speechless trying to assimilate the underlying experience with the current situation. I'm sure they passed it off as me being grief stricken (which I was), but all I could manage to do was point to my dad.

As my gaze swung around to him, I noticed he too looked stunned; perhaps he was having a similar reaction to this "kindred soul"—seeing his sad blue eyes, I grounded myself and took control.

I answered their questions coherently as they "reality tested" Beth, asking if she knew the date. Her answer was May 8th 1917. Everyone looked concerned, and more so when I reported that was the day she was born.

The younger doctor stepped over to me and began explaining they would have to admit her for observation; tears streamed down my face, partly because I was scared but also because I knew him. I knew his soul. Intuitively, I believed he'd come to help our family, but help with what—his presence was calming yet foreboding—was this the beginning of the end?

The day was a lot to take in. Father and I stayed as long as we could, then sadly went home. Many challenging months went by; our dear mother never made it home from the hospital. She passed over the morning before Thanksgiving.

Sun bled through the windows at dawn. I'd been awake for a long time, staring aimlessly at luminous beams draping the wall. I rose and wandered down to the kitchen. I decided to sprinkle nuts out in the yard for the animals so Father would have something to focus on while we ate breakfast.

Standing by the window watching squirrels and blue jays gather for the feast, I felt Beth's presence beside me ... as I turned to look, I was pulled out of my body and we were floating over the backyard in the blink of an eye. I was not afraid, for I felt my mother beside me. I followed her lead: we merged first with the squirrel, his tiny jaws gnawing methodically on a nut, then with the blue jay, and I felt its fast-beating heart and saw through its eyes the uniquity of the yard unfolding before me. We soared to the back of the property and blended with a giant pine; I felt my deep earthy connection with the planet—timeless, endless, and alive throughout eternity.

I was present with each expression of life, edgeless, limitless ... yet, aware of my own consciousness and that of my mom's. "Death" took on new meaning. Those brief moments of lightness were overwhelmingly blissful and familiar; there was an ecstasy of unification between myself and all creations; the animals, plants, earth and the sky were one encompassing field of the same essential energy. I instantly understood much about the way of animals and how they draw knowledge from an infinite source beyond time.

In the background, I heard footsteps coming down the stairs. I whooshed back to my body by the kitchen window. Tears streaming down my cheeks, I was speaking out loud as my father entered the room, "Well, okay, now I know …". Right on queue, he queried, "Know what?" I turned and looked at him, still embraced by the miraculous, and said with a wondrous smile, "Do you really want to know?" "Of course," he replied not knowing what he was in for.

So, gently I relayed the revelatory experience I just had with Beth. His bright blue eyes looked encouraged as he pointed to the squirrel still munching before us. "So, you two merged with that squirrel right there?" "Yes, that was the one." He beamed as he said, "Yes, I can see her there."

Gretta & Saraina with Montserrat & Luna

Cougar Mountain

Beautiful Luna, a small Shepard with a disposition so sweet, was
Gretta's dear friend and companion to my friend Montserrat.
We loved visiting Montserrat's amazing house in the wooded
hills with sweeping views of water, mountains and two cities.
There, we walked for hours through fairy glades and waterfalls,
in perfect harmony.

One evening, we dashed over to their house for a walk after
work. Time slipped away; the rays of sun grew long, saturating
the forest with "magic light". Photographers know it as day's
concession to night—hues illuminated and intensified by the
angle of light before sunset. That's the physics of it, but you
must bathe in the luminosity of the landscape to truly understand.

We were in our own bubble, golden light draping every leaf
and fern—an electric green canopy with azure peeking through.
The edge of darkness crept in; forest sounds shifted with the

light. Gretta and Luna pranced ahead; we saw them slow, stop and look up. "The girls see something," I blurted. "Oh wow, I wonder what it is," quizzed Montserrat, "it could be a deer or coyote—the animals are coming out, this is their time."

We glanced at each other feeling like trespassers in the twilight. Quickly catching up to the dogs, we followed their gaze up, up, to a majestic spotted owl—our mouths dropped. He was hooting. A reply echoed behind us—another owl, slightly smaller, hooting to a baby owl on our right. The dogs did not bark but sat in silence looking up at the blinking owl. We turned slowly in a circle—the owls formed a triangle around us—father, mother and young—could it be?

What privilege allowed us to be in the center of this regal family? We stood reverently in their presence till there was barely enough light to make it to the car. Then respectfully, we walked out of their space, thanking the owls for allowing us to be there. Then we raced down the hill giggling in the darkness.

On the way home, I marveled at the mystical exchange in the forest. I hurried to my library to research Native American symbolism for "Owl Medicine". Low and behold, the owl is associated with clairvoyance, astral projection and magic—owl comes to those who would develop their powers of observation and intuition.[10] I fell asleep thanking the owls for their gift.

Snowflakes from Blue Sky

Early on Easter morning, Gretta and I headed east, anxious to hit the trail; Luna and Montserrat welcomed us and we headed for the waterfall. The forest was still sleeping, silent except for our laughter and the scamper of feet. We hiked straight to the falls. "The girls" waded in the crystal pools below, lapping chilly waters. We sat above on the bridge, feet dangling, admiring the scene. Montserrat decided I should say a few words of gratitude for the richness of our lives and our beloved companions. I reflected a moment, then began speaking from my heart. A few words came out, then I stopped mid-sentence: "Are those real?" "WHAT??" Big, lace-like snowflakes drifted down around our dogs.

"What else could they be?"

"I don't know, but it's not even cold."

In amazement we looked up—the sky was clear blue, cloudless. How was this happening? They were not falling on us, just our dogs. Gretta snapped one and Luna sniffed the air, then they were gone.

We checked in with each other—yes, we were awake, we both saw them, they must have been real. Walking back, we passed a few hikers, so we queried them, "Did you see any snow flakes this morning?" They looked at us funny, "No—did you?"

"Oh, just a few a by the waterfall ... anything is possible there."

Fire-walk with Me

The Readiness is All

—*William Shakespeare*

Montserrat was always coming up with clever new ways to explore consciousness; this time she invited me to a fire-walk. I was excited to go watch! We arrived at the home of Mike, who hosted fire-walks on his property every weekend. Folks were kind and welcoming, with a genuine interest in their eyes as they greeted us.

We bonded easily with the group, singing, dancing and sharing tears of joy as they relayed profound, life-changing experiences. The resounded message: "What one can do, all can do, for we are one". The vibration was *high*!

Miraculous feats were performed; members of the "tribe" walked barefoot on broken glass, bent rebar with their necks—it was mind-bending to say the least. Time was nonexistent. Folded into a space of loving connection, sorrows laid aside, the past forgotten—the present had arrived!

Pitch black heavens beckoned us outdoors, starry gems spun silvery shadows on the landscape with their piercing light; reality was shifting around us. Florid coals spread in sacred ritual began the initiation of the "fire tribe," and we were members by association. What one can do, all can do…. the feeling was palpable and *alive!*

The first walker appeared on the edge of the white-hot bed, all eyes on him. Consciously, deliberately, he strutted the length of the coals, arms thrust to the sky. We cheered, and a parade followed—joyfully they pranced, danced and rolled somersaults over the field of hot coals.

From the sidelines, I reveled in a radical psychic space where the normal laws of reality where miraculously suspended by belief.

A pixie of a woman traversed with an ease and grace so stunning that before I knew it, I was on my feet moving toward her. I greeted her, saying, "If you will hold my hand, I know I can match your energy and walk the coals." Graciously, she bowed, extended her hand and said, "I would be most honored!"

Without hesitation, we were off—our steps in perfect sync—surrounded by the sultry glow. The embers were neither hot nor cold; they felt like Styrofoam peanuts under my feet! Eight giddy strides across—Hazzad!

We landed on the luscious, deep grass, cold and wet—our feet were certainly working now. Dancing like wild poodles, our excitement was shared by all, especially Montserrat who had no idea that I decided to walk until she saw me prancing past—SURPRISE!

Riding high on the energy, we stayed a few more hours then headed for a musical benefit our friends were hosting for the local monastery and battered women's shelter.

To say my mind was altered is an understatement. I was encouraged, enlivened and in love with all things. The potency of the experience flowed through my veins, and out my fingertips.

Inside the hall, I carried it into the dance, smiling at my beautiful brothers and sisters, dancing with the whole room in a new spirit of unity.

As I lay beside Gretta meditating into morning, many pieces of the puzzle connected for me that night. The abstract nature of quantum physics felt reasonably concrete. We believed the coals would not burn us and they didn't, although by every natural law of the physical plane they should have. Some of the walkers stated their intentions aloud, addressing the coals as living participants in a request not to be burned; others spoke to a higher power, asking permission for safe transport.

I simply believed I could do it. Although my motivation in that moment was passionately fueled by faith, my underlying logic came from the belief that potential outcomes lie in waves of probability—a system of superposition that collapses to one result consistent with the observer's belief and intention.[11] I reflected on the words of Ralph Blum from The Book of Runes: *"For even more than doers, we are deciders. And once the decision is clear, the doing becomes effortless."*

Precious Gretta

Dark Night of the Soul

You must push yourself beyond your limits, all the time.

—*Carlos Castaneda*

The phrase "dark night of the soul" originally comes from the writings of Saint John of the Cross in the sixteenth century. His teachings explain the "dark night of the soul" as a spiritual phenomenon (which comes in an episode or episodes) that is named as the second Divine purgation to sear off the imperfections that infect a soul. The subject feels as if the shadow of Hell passes over them.[12]

The most difficult part of pet ownership is that we live longer than they do. My beloved Gretta helped me survive the loss of my sweet parents and my middle sister. So steadfast was her love in the midst of sorrow, I found a way to go on celebrating life even in the face of death.

One morning, curled up together, I awoke to the distinct sensation of Gunnar's spirit sweeping through the house; I literally felt him kiss us on his way to the other side. It was confirmed: Gunnar passed over that day at the age of 17.

A month later, Gretta fell ill; I was grief-stricken as I drove to see her at the hospital during my lunch break. In an attempt to get her to eat, I pulled into the market to buy her some roasted chicken. When I returned to my car, on the pavement in front of my door lay a Rosary with beautiful indigo beads—the image of the sacrificed Christ on the cross hit me in the pit of my stomach. I sensed things were not going to be alright this time; Spirit was gently reminding me we are not our bodies. Gretta passed over that evening at midnight.

There was not enough time to prepare myself for such a loss; If affected me more than anything I could have imagined. It was Gretta's gentle energy that helped me cope and maintain balance through so many hardships. Her sudden death was the proverbial bottom dropping out. For the first time in my life I was seriously despondent; I saw her angelic face in the clouds, trees and the embers of the fire. Like my Mother, she was all things in every moment. I sensed her presence everywhere, yet missed her profoundly.

Dreaming

o o o o o o o o o o o o o o o o o o o o o o o o o o

The breeze at dawn has secrets to tell you ...
Don't go back to sleep

—Rumi

If you want to connect with another being (living or beyond), dreams are miraculous mechanisms—mainlines to the Divine—a glimpse into the limitless potential of our souls.

Sharing dreams was quite normal around our house. My sisters, Torii and Mary, slept in bunk beds. At breakfast, Torii would often describe some colorful dream she had and then discover it mirrored the storyline in a book Mary was reading above her as she slept.

In times of crisis, I always count on my dreams for assistance. For example, five days before my father passed, I experienced a vivid dream: he and Mother (recently deceased) were getting "re-married". I saw their faces, beaming as they looked into each other's eyes. After 56 years together, side by side is where they wanted to be. When I awoke, my inner sense told me it was precognitive (predictive of the future), not metaphorical. Bravely, I shared the story with my sisters; we wined and dined him (more than usual), knowing his time was near. When he slipped over gently in his sleep on the summer solstice, we were at peace. The radiant look on his face told us that all was well.

So it came as no surprise that during the tumultuous period after the loss of Gretta, I had an incredibly lucid, precognitive dream. I was walking in a room full of puppies—every shape and kind imaginable. I was searching aimlessly for her, but there were so many pups and they all looked so appealing; it was overwhelming. I stood in the midst of the wagging bodies and wailed, "Which one are you, where are you, please?!"

Then—up she jumped and landed right on my shoulder; as she passed me in the air, I saw her in detail: she was all white with orange patches on her eyes and a distinct orange spot on one side.

"Is that you?!" I exclaimed. She replied, "Yes, of course, it's me!"

"Are you coming back?"

"Yes."

"In this form?"

"Yes"

"What would you like to be called?"

Her response sounded like Lyla or Lylin, but I was already waking up from all the excitement.

Ecstatic, I woke my partner to share the incredible news with him. "I just saw Gretta, I just saw Gretta; she's white and orange, perhaps a Jack Russell or some sort of Spaniel. She's coming back for sure, I was lucid; it was very vivid!"

Bless his heart, he believed me completely and replied, "Well, let's keep our eyes open for her, she should be landing soon!"

The following weekend we took a trip to a quaint shopping spot north of the city—a group of unique stores set among wooden sidewalks, ponds, a waterwheel and peacocks called the Country Village. Feeling better after my recent contact with Gretta, I wandered into one of the cozy stores. Right in front of me was a beanie-baby dog identical to the dog in the dream (with brown spots, not orange). I know it sounds a bit strange, but it looked so much like the dog in the dream, I had to buy it.

I walked out of the store to show my partner; he was talking on the phone with his mom. As he looked up he said, "Oh, Saraina just found a Gretta look-alike, now she's happy."

Having friends and family who totally believe you when things like this happen is the greatest gift in the world.... boy, am I lucky!

The beanie baby's name was "Bart"—he was a comfort to me for the next two months as I waited.

Triumphant Return

o o o o o o o o o o o o o o o o o o o o o o o o o

Learning is the very essence of humility

—*J. Krishnamurti*

November's pale sun glinted through topaz sky, bouncing off yellow leaves and brown limbs. I drank in the beauty as I sped along the main road near my home. We had just returned from a conference on Long Island. I checked in with myself and noticed gratefully that I felt rested and relaxed. Then, BOOM: a sign in the window of a local pet shop, reading "New puppies just arrived".

I drive this road often, but had never noticed this pet shop. Scanning the skyline, I saw it was five blocks away from the hospital where Gretta met her demise 7 months before.

I raced home and jumped out of my work clothes. "Come on, come on." I said in a pleading tone meant to convince my honey to come with me to the pet shop. I was all excited; I felt Gretta's presence as I read the sign. I wanted to go get her and bring her home!

We zipped over to the pet store; I jumped out of the car and rushed through the door. I began by looking in kennels at the front of the shop: first kennel—no, second kennel—no, third kennel—no … then I heard the words, "Saraina, she's right *here!*"

My partner was pointing across the room at an all-white puppy with orange patches on his eyes and a big orange spot on his side—the cutest Jack Russell you could ever imagine! He recognized the pup simply from my description in the dream!

I rushed over and reached into the open top cage. All the other pups were sleeping in a happy heap, but not this one. He was wide-awake, up on his back legs, clawing the wire fence madly to get my attention. I snatched him up in my arms and hugged him to my chest while he licked my face. He was wriggling all over—head, tail and toe.

I stood in astonishment and relief, reeling from the magnitude of the miracle that just occurred. We were giddy! Finally, my partner asked, "Did you bring your checkbook?" I answered, "Of course!"

So home we went, with the adorable pup whose tag identified him as "Burt" (remember the beanie dog was Bart). I set up his bowls, gave him a little bath, wrapped him in a towel, held him in my arms and cried tears of pure joy.

At last, basking in the glow of gratitude, we snuggled in bed and slept like the most blessed angels in heaven.

Soon after Lylin's arrival a spectacular rainbow graced our home!

Lylin's first day

Lylin McFarland

To see a world in a grain of sand and heaven in a flower
Hold infinity in the palm of your hand
And eternity in an hour

—*William Blake*

In the morning, still grinning from the astounding circumstances of Lylin's arrival, I reminisced over the past several months: the precognitive dream with Gretta, the Beanie Baby dog, and two months of unwavering faith, silently awaiting her return. What a glorious lesson in the art of attraction; I felt deeply blessed and overwhelmingly thankful.

Lylin joined our clan effortlessly. He was beyond handsome and his perky spirit and "can do" personality was pure healing after the long period of mourning.

We resumed our weekend travels in our motor home, heading north or east depending on the weather. Exploring, hiking and swimming—we were having a blast!

Before long, we tested the newbie's intuitive savvy. I was throwing a floating ring into the shallows of Rattlesnake Lake, and he fetched it gleefully—he loved water instantly. Inadvertently, I flung the wrong ring, which didn't float, and it promptly sunk. It was sitting on the bottom about six inches deep. Lylin was trying to retrieve it blowing bubbles out his nose and diving in again and again, but it wasn't quite working for him. Then my partner and I both had the same idea: he should drag it with his paw. We sent the picture and—presto—he did it! This generated rounds of clapping and laughter, which served to bolster his fetching spirit! He was sharp as a whip and very spunky.

By now I had successfully transitioned from systems administration to vocational consulting. I'd been working as an instructor and counselor at a local college. Since Lylin returned as a Jack Russell, I knew it was time to give self-employment serious thought. Having lived with a terrier before, I fully understood that they don't take well to isolation, nor did I want to be gone long hours anymore.

After fifteen years of working a full-time job and maintaining a private practice, I was ready to shift!

Still, I wondered whether I could actually maintain my income from my practice alone. The thought of doing what I love all day was enticing, but the risk was daunting.

I found myself having an internal debate on the issue while walking the hills with my precious new companion. Suddenly I stopped and asked Spirit directly: "Should I quit my job and pursue my practice? Sure my astrologer says I can do it, but she doesn't have to pay my mortgage. Please, please, show me a sign of what I should do!"

I walked on through the drizzle, and after several blocks I came upon a card lying in the rain on the sidewalk in front of me. It was the size of a business card, and it had something written on it:

"Good Shepard of our souls and bodies, from age to age you have led your people in the paths of righteousness and truth for your own name's sake.
Through the years of our lives you have guided us faithfully into green pastures and beside still waters and restored our souls.
Through the blood of your eternal covenant you furnish us with every good thing in order that we accomplish your will and do that which is pleasing your sight.
Our cup of blessing runs over …"

There was more to the prayer; I finished reading, turned it over and grinned from ear to ear. There was a fabulous colored picture of Christ carrying a bedraggled soul on his shoulders, while walking on water.

I looked up and shouted, "Thank you! I'm taking this as a YES!" I promptly quit my job.

Lylin meets his double—look at that smile!

A sign from Spirit—time to take a leap of faith!

The Sorcerer's Apprentice

The Sorcerer's Apprentice

o o o o o o o o o o o o o o o o o o o o o o o o o o o
The sense of Unity is the core of true service

—*N. Sri Ram*

According to Dr. Wayne Dyer, a "sorcerer" is simply "one who is connected to Source". And since this is my intention, both in life and in work, I gratefully accept this title. Lylin, who attends all sessions in my private practice, is aptly nicknamed "The Sorcerer's Apprentice."

One day Lylin (still a puppy) nibbled on a client's sandal while in session. It was time to have a heart-to-heart talk. I told him in a serious tone that he was there to assist me, not distract me. Then I explained further that my practice is what pays for everything we have, including lovely dog toys and treats. Apparently, he took our discussion literally; shortly thereafter, he began to participate, adding his "healing perspective" to the session when appropriate.

The work day starts early around our house. Clients are in different time zones, so we rise to meet their schedules. My "furry alarm" knows just when an unscheduled client is going to call—"Sergeant Lylin" arrives bedside with his own form of reveille. First, he simply stares at me to wake up. If I choose to ignore this subtle message, he moves to the next level: a paw on the bed, pushing emphatically into the mattress—wake up, wake up—while tipping his head quizzically—why aren't you up?!

In the beginning, I merely thought he wanted me to let him out. So periodically I would pull the covers over my head and pretend to ignore him. This brought forth the terrier tactic with the most bravado: digging me out of bed relentlessly.

Soon I understood there were more complex motives behind his actions: when he wanted me out of bed for a client, he would not go outside but rather return to his bed once I was up and awake. Sure enough, a client always called within 20 minutes of my rousing.

Due to the loyal diligence of my apprentice, I'm conscious enough to take the call with a cup of tea in hand!

Time Keepers

One of the greatest joys of being self-employed is that you call the shots; you decide when and where to work, and your dog *can* attend. I've always allowed my dogs in the office with clients; they have a calming presence that I feel benefits them.

When I first opened my practice, I was so grateful to actually have clients that it was easy to go overtime. This was counterproductive, as I was only paid for an hour. I needed to work on ensuring that the client was complete and ready to go out the door in 60 minutes.

Both Gretta and Lylin took an avid interest in tending to time. Gretta started the process by walking over to the client exactly one hour from when the session began and laying her head gently on their knee as if to say, "It's been lovely, but you should wrap it up now."

Lylin continued this practice with a bit more color: he would pop up on the hour, walk to the side of the client's chair, pawing gently to get their attention, then make soft woofing sounds or just stare at them with his head tipped in a curious expression, "Will you be leaving soon?"

Fortunately, most clients find this amusing and it gives me an opportunity to say; "Oh my, look at the time, we really must conclude."

One woman was making fabulous progress when Lylin "visited" her, so she requested another half hour. I happily agreed and reported the news by saying, "Go lay down please; we're going another 30 minutes." Back to his bed he went, but he was up again in exactly 30 minutes, giving her "the look". And this time, he was sure she'd be leaving.

My client was so amused by his routine that as she walked to her car, she turned and quipped, "Are ya happy now?" In response, he wagged his tail from the porch as if to say "Yep, quite happy, do come again!"

So, my furry apprentices have trained me to adhere to my own professional standards; start on time, end on time.

Case Study #1
Loves Heals Melissa

Inside my soothing, lavender office, the session began. Lylin positioned himself in his cushy, brown-velvet bed. He was gnawing busily on a chew when Melissa began to cry over the death of her daughter. Her emotions overflowed; we felt the profoundness of her sorrow. As her silent witness, I was at a loss for words; how does one begin to ease the suffering from such a tragedy?

Lylin, however, didn't hesitate to try. Before I could offer a tissue, he dropped his treat and rushed to her, gently; he stood on his sturdy back legs and placed a paw on her knee, tipping his head in query, "I see you're suffering; what can I do to help?"

Seeing his look of concern, Melissa managed a small smile, but her grief was too deep to arrest the tears. Undaunted, he rushed out of the office, returning momentarily with his favorite toy: a small, furry chipmunk which he placed on her lap as an offering of condolence.

The kindness of his gesture brought forth an unexpected giggle, followed by a genuine beam of joy to Melissa's tear-streaked face; she reached for the pooch who needed no further invitation—up he went to a cozy spot on her lap where he could tuck his paw around her neck and enthusiastically lick away her tears. In just a few moments of loving contact, healing occurred; the pain receded temporarily and gratitude shone through.

I remained silent, sensing his innate wisdom. For truly Lylin was more effective with his actions than I could ever have been with only words.

Case Study #2
Who's wearing the pants around here?

Karla called with a pressing issue and requested a session right away. We greeted her at the door and moved swiftly to the office. Usually a calm, soft-spoken woman in her twenties, she was visibility upset over a love affair gone awry. Her story unfolded; venting her frustration, her cheeks began to redden and her voice was rising out of confusion and dissatisfaction with a recent encounter.

Lylin surveyed her from his bed as her emotions increased to a new level, then quick as a lightening bug, he dashed out of the room (on a mission I feared). I noted his departure, but was immersed in the session.

Moments later, my apprentice reappeared behind Karla. He had something white in his mouth which he was flinging glee-fully—I was terribly curious, but I didn't want to disengage Karla to look. She continued to vent, and Lylin continued to prance; he danced back and forth, swirling his prize is the air, then pouncing on it. Eventually it was too much; my eyes began to dart back and forth between the unaware client and the frol-icking pup. I was desperately trying to maintain my composure and professionalism when I realized that Lylin had unearthed a pair of men's underwear and was whipping them around like prey.

As this realization hit me, Karla, sensing all the movement behind her, turned and stared directly at the "pants". I gulped as her gaze swung back to me. All I could manage to say was; "Those aren't mine!"

Simultaneously, we burst into a fit of laughter; Lylin rushed forward, placing the "forbidden treasure" at her feet—"See! I killed them for you!" Karla, visibly brightened by this humorous event, praised and patted him, affirming his contribution to the session; "Thank-you Lylin, that's the best therapy in the world—shake 'em up and show 'em who's boss!"

Suddenly, I realized I'd been holding my breath; now, I sighed with relief, for once again, the Sorcerer's Apprentice saved the day—Karla left smiling and laughing about the wild and wonderful ways of love.

Case Study #3
Smoking is bad for your health, unless you're a dog!

It was a brilliant autumn day; the warmth of the sun kissed by a gentle breeze made the temperature just right. Fall is my favorite time of year and I live for those glorious days.

Today, I was teaching a workshop for a group of girlfriends. There was just enough time to run to the community market and buy flowers for the table. I was excited to connect with my friends and share new information.

As the women arrived, I hugged each one happily. Lylin showed his enthusiasm by hopping up to kiss them and acting excessively cute. I thought his little tail would wag right off with a house full of women doting on him.

Prior to the workshop, one of the women phoned to ask if Lylin could be in his kennel during the class because she found him distracting. Although I understood her concerns, I gently reminded her that having the workshops at my home greatly reduces the cost for all of us. Kindly, she agreed that he could be free and I agreed to make sure he stayed in the background as much as possible.

Well, when this dear friend arrived, she took off her coat and moved toward the sofa. Lylin spied her, leaped through the air and literally pushed her onto the couch. The surprised woman turned to me and exclaimed, "Did you tell him?" I was as stunned as she was, and stammered, "No, No, I didn't tell him, but he knows everything." "Well I can tell he knows!" She decreed empathically. "He's never greeted me like that before." "Yes, he does seem to sense our conversation; I am very sorry for his behavior." I added, "He'll be going to his cabana for a 'time out' after that little stunt."

So, into the cabana (kennel) he went, facing the group with his lips pressed against the bars, open enough to show his teeth in a sneer of disgust. It was hilarious! He held that pose for twenty minutes while we tried our best not to laugh at his protesting expression.

Finally, we couldn't take it any longer. We decided he should come out and try again with the group. So, out he came, and went straight to his bed, falling soundly asleep as if to say, "This whole affair has drained me!"

Patricia, one of the guests that day, is a smoker. I believe she is the only smoker I know. When she comes for sessions she takes a smoke break in the back yard and plays fetch with Lylin.

As it came time to take our break, I started my wrap-up of the past two hours. Just as I said, "Ok, let's take a break." I looked down to see Lylin sitting on the carpet, facing Patricia with her cigarette pack and lighter in his mouth. So I added, "And go smoke." This got everyone's attention and they howled at how clever he was to have woken up, snuck over to the cigarettes and made it back right on cue.

Accepting his invitation, Patricia joyfully took the cigarettes and proceeded out to the yard for a happy game of fetch.

Lylin rests at the end of the work day

PART II

Pet-Pourri: A Collection of Short Tales

King of the River

Growing up in a small town in Wyoming, Dennis recalls his German Shepard, Duke, was "King of the River" (on his side). The other side of the very same river was the exclusive domain of Jake, an enormous St. Bernard. The good people of the town often speculated on the outcome if the "two kings" were to meet; would they take it up in a fight or just respect the other's domain and walk on?

Well, as fortune would have it, Dennis and his little sister Cathy were playing by the river the day it came down. Duke was making his usual rounds on the west bank and Jake was following his routine on the east. They spotted each other and froze as if by spell—transfixed on opposing banks, taking in the presence of the other. Silently, they stood for some time, then moved forward in synchronicity, wading into the river until they were swimming to meet in the middle.

Dennis watched anxiously in anticipation; he couldn't believe his eyes. The stiff current barely affected these strong, muscular dogs as they crossed to the center. Treading gently, they stared into each other's eyes for a moment, then touched noses, pausing in acknowledgement. Then, they turned and swam back to their respective banks where they shook off in the sun and wagged a casual goodbye with their tails. The "two kings" had taken the high road, honoring the other's territory for the common good.

Dennis (with Cathy in tow) ran home bubbling with excitement for sharing this fantastic story with his family. This was the stuff legends are made of and they alone were there to witness it. He couldn't wait to share. As he unfolded the tale, his family listened intently, cheering him on with shouts of excitement.

Suddenly, his mother noticed Cathy was missing. Dennis had barely concluded when a frantic question took precedence, "Where's Cathy!" mom exclaimed. No one knew. Everyone scrambled out the door and began combing the area for the missing 2-year-old; they spotted her back on the banks of the river. Duke was with her. Every time she stood to access the river, he nudged her back into the safety of the sand. Her gentle protector was on-duty, standing strong between her and the rapids. Mother ran and swept her into her arms, carting her away from tumbling waters. Duke strode alongside regally with his head held high—after all, he was the "King of the River" (on his side).

Mollie and Big Cat

Big Cat sat on the grassy hill above the farm from sun-up till sun-down, watching for moles. His amazing size and color made him look more like a raccoon than a feline; his large muscular body moved with extraordinary sleekness under his long furry coat. He was a presence to behold as he meditated silently, massive paws folded comfortably, waiting for the next moment on the "Mole Patrol".

Mollie shared the five-acre farm with Big Cat, although they were not close; they each had their own routine and moved in separate orbits except at night when they retreated to the comfort of home and their loving keeper, Crista.

Mollie was a tabby cat, and actually a male mistaken for a "she" at birth. Still, the name fit and he was undaunted by any confusion on his human's part. He was his "own man" and a bit of a culprit.

Crista is what you'd call a "cat person"—she loved cats and usually had several in her life at any given time. A neighbor with a litter of golden labs hoped to sway her to the "dog side"—he brought a pack of wiggling pups to the farm thinking she'd adopt one (or more). The discussion was on-going, but she couldn't be convinced; her kitties were so self-contained and satisfied, a change seemed unwarranted at this time.

As the neighbor retreated with his clan, the weather turned stormy. Mid-afternoon before dusk, fluffy puffs of snow were swirling through the air and blanketing the ground. The wind picked up, chilling temperatures to below freezing—unusual for Northern Oregon this time of year.

Mollie showed up at the door speckled with snow drops. Crista waited for Big Cat to follow, but he didn't. She called from the doorway—visibility was low, barely 20 feet in the mist—the wind spirited the words right off her lips. She listened intently for a reply—any sound or hint of his whereabouts—but all she heard was wind torrents shaking the trees. She closed the door and waited.

Before long, Mollie began pacing and clawing at the door. Crista immediately sensed it was about Big Cat. She threw on her coat and followed him into the night. Mollie led her down the driveway to a stand of giant pines; he placed his paws on one tree mewing loudly into its dark limbs. Crista strained to see through the shroud of fog—again, she called but heard nothing. She walked swiftly back to the house (Mollie followed), returning with a large flashlight to pierce the blackness. Sure enough, 40 feet up clung a terrified Big Cat. Treed by the hounds before the storm hit, he was frozen—too frightened to move for hours.

However, hope was alive—they had contact with one another. Temperature still dropping, her fingers numbed as she patiently spoke words of encouragement to coax him down. Robotically he began to descend, limb by limb, stiffened from exposure and fear; what kept him going was Crista—she would save him from dogs, snow or anything that got in her way. Finally he was within reach. She swept him from the branches into her arms and they ran for the warmth of the hearth with no time to lose.

Big cat was going to be fine; his dense coat protected him long enough for his comrade to bring help, but he would never have survived that night in the tree. Purring softly side by side, they let down their guard and admitted a fondness for each other. Cozy by the fire, the three drank in their victory fueled by intuition and the power of love.

Beautiful Tasha Rose

Tasha Rose

Tasha Rose, a magnificent 145-pound Alaskan Malamute, and her keeper, Jai, enjoyed their daily walk on a logging road overlooking the ocean. As they headed out, clouds raced against endless blue sky, a light breeze beckoned them as they crested the hill where ocean comes into view. Then suddenly without warning, Tasha stopped short, sat down, and wouldn't budge for some unknown reason. Jai was so engrossed in the view and getting exercise, she almost tripped over her "parked pooch".

Surprised and concerned, Jai inquired, "What's up Tasha? This is not like you!" From the look in her eyes it seemed Tasha wanted to go home. At a loss for what made her freeze in her tracks, she tried coaxing her to continue. Still, she remained planted—now on top of Jai's feet! It was a strong message: we shall go no further!

As you can imagine, there's no bargaining with a dog her size; you certainly can't carry her, so reluctantly Jai headed toward home. Tasha hopped up, indicating with a wave of her tail this was the correct choice.

It took 20 minutes on the isolated road to arrive at the edge of their neighborhood. As they reached the first house, a truckload of drunken, gun-toting men came tearing up the gravel lane. Jai turned to look, just as they spotted her and careened in her direction. They began to harass her, but now she was close enough to a neighbor's house to run for safety. Disgruntled, the rowdy men sped off in the direction from which the two had just come.

Catching her breath, Jai immediately understood Tasha's message and most importantly, the miracle that had just occurred. Somehow, Tasha Rose sensed the arrival of dangerous men and knew the exact timing required to turn and head for safety. Jai bent down to hug and nuzzle her faithful companion, who saved them from imminent danger; her timing could not have been any more perfect or her intention any more clear.

Tasha and Jasmin

Our hearty "shero" had an instinctive love for children; it seemed her personal mission was to protect the innocent. When she heard neighbors spanking a child, she rushed over and sniffed the youngster, sending a gentle but firm message: there's always a better way and I'm watching carefully until you find it!

Jai's son and daughter-in-law were visiting her lovely home with grand-daughter Jasmine. The family was winding down after a long day. Jai wandered down the hall to check on them; with a start, she noticed Jasmine was absent. "Where's Jasmine?" she inquired urgently. "We thought she was with you," they replied. They rushed down the corridor calling the missing 3-year-old. What they found sent them into panic: the living room was empty, and the front door ajar. Jai raced out to the expansive yard and spied Jasmine over 100 feet away, walking onto the roadway.

Her quick assessment brought an intense feeling of terror. The road sat on a blind curve, and a car was rounding the bend. Full-on she sprinted toward the child. "Jasmine stop! Get back from the road!" Neither she or her voice could intercept the toddler—the distant was too great. It felt like a bad dream, watching helplessly, unable to intervene.

She sprinted harder, coming close enough to see that Tasha was with Jasmine. Sensing danger, she had followed the exploring child onto the road. As the car swung round the curve, our "shero" grabbed the nape of Jasmine's neck and flung her onto the embankment, barely clearing the roadway in time to save herself.

Time froze; the car sped past, oblivious to the child and dog. Jasmine was crying from the jolt and her rough landing, but she was safe. Tasha rushed over to lick her tears as Jai caught up to comfort her.

Jai had witnessed another miracle from their brave protector—a young life saved, a family kept whole by the selfless guardian who never failed.

Lizzy

Lizzy and Leanne lived an adventurous life in Los Gatos, California. Los Gatos, meaning "The Cat" in Spanish, was a fitting name for the residence of such an elegant feline like Lizzy. A Lynx Point Siamese with definitive taste, Lizzy only came when her keeper whistled Mozart's Ninth—no other Mozart would do and certainly not your basic "come here" whistle could fetch her.

Their cozy cabin sat on six acres above the hills of Los Gatos—they were cheek to cheek with nature; many animals shared their space. The wild birds and bunnies were wonderful, but Leanne worried at times about giving Ms. Lizzy free range in this rural terrain—what if she encountered a coyote or a bob cat? The thought was difficult, but more difficult yet would be to keep Lizzy from exploring this glorious open land. It's true, she was an adventurer, yet she loved her home and the closeness of their connection too much to stray far.

This is why Leanne was alarmed when she didn't return at her usual time this particular evening. The sun was sinking—no Lizzy? All her silent fears came rushing to the forefront, but she knew panic would not serve her if she needed to find her beloved. So she quieted her mind and established a direct connection with Lizzy, who communicated that she was safe, but frightened. The insight was strong enough to have Leanne up and running in her direction—down the pasture, through the woods and thickets, directly to the spot where her stranded Lizzy clung to a high tree limb. She'd been treed by another cat who was a neighborhood bully!

Quickly Leanne organized a rescue via ladder, and before long the two were safely on their way home. They slept tight with all the excitement of the day. Early the next morning, Leanne was sitting in her garden taking in the first rays of light; it was quiet, barely a soul around. Lizzy was with her, sunning her belly blissfully in the grass, when suddenly she sensed the presence of danger! A coyote had crept into their safe haven and was sneaking up on them. Leanne barely had time to react when Lizzy sprang into the air—straight up, mouth open with arms outstretched like a lion—it startled the coyote enough to make it turn tail and run.

Laughing aloud, she praised her proud kitty who fearlessly repelled a wily dog at least six times her size! It was a surprising moment, for both Leanne and the coyote, but it ended her worries about Lizzy's prowess in the wild!

Lizzy and Boog

Before moving to California, Leanne was given a gerbil whom she named Boog. She awoke to the sound of Lizzy fussing like she was looking at a bird, you know, the chattering cats make when they're on the prowl. Before she had a moment to sort it out, Boog came running toward her with Lizzy hot on her tail. She thought the poor gerbil was a goner, but instead they began to play a game of "cat and mouse"; soon the gerbil was chasing Lizzy!

Their friendship grew to a daily routine. When Boog wanted to play, she would sit on top of her running wheel. Lizzy would come over, open the lid with her paw, take Boog by the nape of the neck and drop her on the floor. They'd dash and chase each other around the house until both were tuckered out and retreated for a happy nap.

Folks who happened by couldn't believe their eyes or the amazing amount of trust these fine companions shared for each other—everyone agreed it was a strong argument for intelligence ruling over instinct!

Lizzy and Abby

As Leanne entered the living room one day, Lizzy was staring out the window with great intensity. Immediately she sensed her concern, so she rushed over to look: a momma cat with five tiny babies! Someone had abandoned her and Lizzy tuned right in.

Joyfully, they welcomed the orphaned family into their home; everyone cooperated to raise five healthy kittens, and each was placed in a wonderful home.

The mother cat remained with Leanne and Lizzy for the rest of her days (over ten years). They named her Abby. She became Lizzy's best friend and a valued member of their family.

Lady and the Book

The Skagit Valley in spring is one of our favorite destinations; the rainbows of tulips surrounding the tiny town of La Conner are stunning. Having soaked up as much radiant color as we could amidst the flowering fields, we wandered through town, window-shopping and chatting with fellow dog owners along the way. Gretta, my beautiful Weimaraner, was enjoying the day with us.

A lively woman struck up a conversation about her dog Lady—she was the same breed and extremely intelligent. She relayed the most fascinating account of Lady's behavior while she and a colleague were having a philosophical discussion over a cozy cup of tea one afternoon. The conversation reached a point where both women were trying to remember the name of a book pertinent to the topic. "It was one of those moments where you have the title on the tip of your tongue, but just can't bring it to mind," she said. They even got up and perused her bookshelves trying to identify the book.

Lady was dozing in a pool of sunlight streaming through a nearby window; she sat up and took notice, then gracefully resumed her position.

Eventually, the two women ventured off for some shopping. Returning several hours later, to their wonderment they found "the book" on the foot stool of her favorite chair.

They were ecstatic to find the elusive title, and then they became mystified as the reality of its appearance took hold. How could it be? No one heard the conversation; no one had been in the house except for her beloved canine. Lady wagged over to her, prancing lightly foot to foot, seeming to profess her success in producing the book. All evidence indicated that Lady had indeed plucked the book from the bookshelf herself and carried it to the footstool in a gesture of service. It was most unusual, the woman reflected, "but I'm quite sure she did it—who knows, she may have even read it before we returned!"

Zeb strums Larry's guitar!

Zebulon

Zebulon was found in an alley at a mere 5 weeks of age; he was solid grey with mesmerizing green eyes. The fine folks who rescued him already had three cats, so they asked Julie and Larry if they would give him a home. Graciously they obliged and Zebulon, or "Zeb" as he came to be known, was welcomed into their home.

Julie recalls Zeb as incredibly bright, playful and full of life—a trickster. He turned ordinary experiences into frisky games.

First, there was the "bed-making game": each morning as Julie entered the bedroom, he would leap up, coiled in excitement, waiting for her to throw pillows. He wiggled on the bed as they launched, then sprang forth like Zorro to catch them mid-flight. He'd ride those pillows down in victory; the fact that they were three times his size didn't hamper him. He pounced, she giggled, the more she giggled the higher he'd spring. He was a comedian in a cat's body!

Indeed, generating laughter was his natural talent and ambition—he'd strum Larry's guitar in the evening while they dined. After dinner he'd entertain them with his mouse on a bungee, pulling it as far as he could then releasing it so he could run and catch it in the other room about 6 feet in the air. They watched him for hours—the TV became extinct.

After his keepers retired for the evening, he'd spend time hiding things in their shoes so they'd find his offerings as they left for work the next day. He was a busy little jester!

Having successfully cheered his family on to their workdays, he would stroll out to the yard, stationing himself under the hedge which borders the sidewalk.

Silently he'd wait there for unsuspecting walkers. As soon as they were within range, he'd rush out, bat their feet and dash back under the bushes. First there were shrieks of surprise, then laughter as folks caught a glimpse of Zeb running for cover.

Situated on a common walking route down to Laguna Beach, Zeb got lots of action. People found him so amusing they'd return with unsuspecting friends just to watch them leap with surprise. He was known throughout the neighborhood as a feline prankster. Around four months of age he created a new routine; going neighbor to neighbor each day for a visit. When he failed to return one evening, Larry and Julie went searching; sure enough a neighbor unsuspectingly adopted him thinking he was a stray.

To ensure this never happened again, they bought him a collar with a special tag detailing his name and phone number. He wore it for about a week before it went missing.

Julie told Zeb he couldn't go outside until he had his collar on—they looked all over the house, under the bed, every nook and cranny, thinking he had lost it inside the house. There was no sign of the collar.

The door bell rang; a customer of Julie's came to drop off vintage photos for retouching. As she opened the door, Zeb shot out like a rocket. Standing on the porch talking to her client, she could see him from afar running up the hill with something in his mouth. It was his collar! He returned to porch, dropped his collar at her feet, and rolled over on his back as if to say, "Please, put it on so I go can play!"

Julie had to stop the conversation and fill her customer in at this point, it was too astounding not to share; neither could believe what had just happened. Knowing his collar wasn't in the house, he had taken his only chance to run down the hill, pick it up and bring it back.

Now he could happily resume his rounds, greeting his public and generating smiles in the 'hood.

Dawn the Wake-Up Dog

At a quaint bed & breakfast near Milwaukee, Helen and her family had the privilege of meeting Dawn. Snuggled beneath vintage comforters in their cozy cabin, they heard a scratching at first light. Helen listened intently, and there it was again: scratch, scratch, scratch ... she hoisted her robe over her shoulders, strode to the door, and opened it to find a jolly retriever wagging "good morning" on the porch.

Pleasantly surprised, she greeted Dawn, who after a few pats pranced along to the next cabin, raised her paw ... scratch, scratch, scratch. The door opened quickly, then they too were greeted by the smiley lab; they too thanked her generously for the call.

Helen watched as Dawn continued her rounds, rousing each occupant in turn. It was amusing to watch the varying responses—some guests had been there before, others stood mystified and gazing half awake.

As it turns out, Dawn began her practice some years ago while her keeper cooked up the morning fare. Wanting to be of service and enjoy a meal too, she began her ritual wake-up call for breakfast, which, thanks to Dawn, is always served piping hot and perfectly on time!

Beeker

Beeker was a walking kind of kitty—he dutifully patrolled the neighborhood keeping everything in check. A large, cuddly boy with tuxedo markings, he took his job as escort very seriously, ushering the children to the bus stop each day without fail. He'd wait till they boarded, then at the end of the day he'd stroll over anticipating their return.

Halloween was Beeker's favorite holiday; he especially enjoyed going door to door with the family and dog. He participated fully until they came to the end of his territory … there he stopped for fear of crossing paths with neighboring felines. He did not appreciate the fact that the rest of the clan moved on with the dog. He'd stand right on the invisible boundary and yowl with discontent as the little "treaters" trudged forward. As soon as their bags were filled, they'd swing back to where Beeker waited, tail twitching impatiently. The very minute they crossed over to his turf, he'd rush up and bat the dog's muzzle—punishment for letting them stray into unprotected terrain. He followed this routine diligently for 14 years; he was a model cat citizen!

In his senior years, he didn't hesitate to state his point of view, even more vehemently than in his youth. He took to spraying the closet in the daughter's room, and at first no one understood why. Mother, Pat, quickly contacted her trusted pet intuitive who reported that a young man was literally rubbing Beeker's fur the wrong way!

Pat brought the news back to the family for feedback. Sure enough, she was absolutely correct: the daughter's boyfriend always brushed Beeker's fur against the grain when he said "hello"—although the boyfriend thought he liked it, he didn't!

The closet contained the boyfriend's suit from prom night; Beeker went right to it and sprayed to get his point across expediently. Once the message was translated and the improper petting was curtailed, the spraying ceased immediately.

Mico

Mico was a clever dog—a large, friendly Rottweiler with an easy-going attitude. Not much bothered him. He and his keeper, Corrina recently moved to a new house in West Hollywood after she landed a job as a technical artist. They were enjoying their new digs until the temps began to rise, then they noticed the windows on their stylish bungalow were painted shut.

As Northwest natives, neither of them had a taste for hot weather; Corrina ordered an air conditioner straight away. However, Mico didn't wait around for solutions; he quickly mastered the handle on the refrigerator. She came home to find him sitting contentedly with his head inside the nice cool Westinghouse! He never ate the food—nope, he just wanted to enjoy the frosty crispness of the frigid air.

Which he did, every day until the two headed back to Seattle where a woof can enjoy a cool breeze and an invigorating dip in the lake!

Samantha the "En-Chantress"

There are cat lovers and then there is Brian—his first cat had his own checking account. It's obvious that he sees cats' superior intelligence and fully honors their innate abilities!

This is why their cozy home is known as the "kitty ranch". He and wife Jane have hearts bigger than Montana ... never would they turn away a soul in need. When neighbors moved and abandoned their cats, they'd be welcomed and loved on "the ranch". Even cats with health concerns whom no one else wanted were a treasure in their eyes; for truly they are, each little spirit has so much life and love to give.

Brian adopted Samantha at a Renaissance fair. She was a striking Calico with absolutely perfect markings; they clicked immediately and began the most amazing friendship.

Samantha was a scout: the eyes and ears of the neighborhood. She'd scale the ladder to the rooftop on her daily watch, surveying the terrain, waiting for visitors or family to come by so she could chat. A Gemini by birth, she was highly communicative! She had a greeting or a sound for every exchange with each person; she developed her own kitty cat language.

She knew exactly when Brian would be headed home from a business trip; she'd ask Jane to let her out, then sit on the porch awaiting her beloved keeper. She was accurate within 30 minutes every time. As soon as Brian arrived, she'd escort him to the bedroom so he could greet her properly with strokes and kisses. Then, once his bags were on the floor and their greeting complete, she'd race around the house inviting him to catch her. He'd chase her one direction, then she'd do a switch-back and they'd run wildly the other way. She honored this ritual throughout her life.

When Brian wasn't traveling, he worked at home. Samantha loved those days. She'd follow his morning routine from start to finish, and once he settled into work she'd find her spot on the bed and nap. Unless of course the curtains were closed, in which case she'd march out and chirp her friendly request for "sunshine on the bed, please", then settle down and sleep until the phone rang.

Brian always answered his calls with an official greeting—"Hello, this is Brian". As soon as she heard him say it, she would scamper to his office and chant his name:

B R I A N—B R I A N—B R I A N—albeit a meowing version, the actual word "Brian" was discernable and distinct enough that callers on the other end could hear it. Many would inquire, "Is someone calling you ... do you have to go?" Imagine the response when he replied "No, it's just my cat!" So, on and on she'd go chanting his name until he got off the phone and was all hers, once again.

In the evening, Jane and Brian would take a leisurely walk to the nearby market, and Samantha would follow. She'd prance 4-5 paces ahead then wait as they caught up, prance, prance, prance, then wait, all the way up to the street where she'd stop completely so they could cross safely together. While they shopped, she waited dutifully, then they'd prance back home all together.

This beloved feline lived 21 years, surviving many a health crisis through the miracle of their love. Her sweet presence is still strongly felt; each night as they drift off to sleep, they feel her spirit jump on the bed and settle beside them; a bond of love undaunted by death.

Angel Comes Home

A lovely woman named Jeanette came to me after hearing the story of Gretta's return. Her beloved collie, Angel, past over—she wondered if I could assist her in determining whether she intended to return to her and if so, when.

I was hesitant, as I prefer not to predict the future. I adhere to the laws of quantum physics, which illustrate that reality is continuously unfolding moment to moment in waves of possibility. Only when the observer decides on a course of action do waves lock into solid particles and create an outcome which matches the expectations of the observing force.[11]

Predicting the future creates an ethical dilemma for me: I consider it "dicey business" as you run the risk of programming someone into creating your version of a future, which lies only in probability.

I highly respect and admire Albert Einstein. However, I disagree with his argument against quantum theory whereby he says: "God does not play dice"[15]—I believe God *does* play dice in the sense that you get to *roll your own*.

After a moment of reflection, I shared my concerns about predictions. She agreed completely, yet her hopeful look convinced me it was worth a try. She clarified: she wasn't looking for a prediction as much as a connection with her animal friend on the other side.

I said a blessing for the session, quieted my mind and ask for communication with Angel. She was happy to oblige; I could see her vividly in my mind's eye. I described her appearance to be sure I had indeed connected with her beloved spirit. She confirmed this was "her girl," so I proceeded, asking how she was and if she had designs on returning to an incarnation on Earth. The immediate answer was: "Yes!" she had planned to return and showed me a "picture" of what she would look like.

I described her new appearance to Jeanette with as much detail as I could: an adorable fluffy dog, perhaps a Border Collie or Akita.

Jeanette was encouraged, but added, "I am not familiar with either of those dogs, don't they have pointy ears? I don't like pointy ears."

Laughing, I suggested she go home and look them up and let Angel know which she preferred. "Where will I find her?" she asked. I replied, "She will be in a home far north of Seattle, but don't worry, she'll find you."

That was all the information I received, so we concluded our session. Seven months passed (and I'd completely forgotten our session) when I met Jeanette at a conference. We hugged and chatted as we set up our booths. Once my booth was in order, I floated out into the room to mingle, reconnect with friends, and share recent adventures and revelations.

I was admiring the beautiful display and fabulous products of Sylvee, an herbalist, when she handed me a photo of a puppy. Her purebred Miniature Australian Shepherd recently had pups with the Border Collie next door: one puppy had not been spoken for. He was completely cute and cuddly; I loved him at first glance. My immediate response was, "Oh he'd make a perfect little brother for Lylin!" Then my better judgment (and his price tag) made me think twice.

I chatted my way back around to where Jeanette was sitting at her booth. She sat quietly and I detected an undertone of sadness. I walked up and asked, "What ails you, my dear?" "Well, I still haven't connected with Angel and it's been 7 months. I thought I would have seen her by now." Suddenly it dawned on me, "Oh my Goodness! Follow me sister, I think things are looking up!"

I grabbed Jeanette and sped her over to Sylvee's booth, then I placed the puppy photo in her hand, not saying a word. I watched her face carefully as she took in the image of the small furry face. First, she looked astonished, then elated as she shrieked, "It's her, it's her, I can feel it—it is my Angel!" She added that three nights before she'd dreamt about a puppy, who wanted his name to be Michael.

Slyvee looked pleased by this news, but had no idea what we were talking about. Hugging one another excitedly, we shared the story of how Jeanette had been waiting for contact from a Border Collie—*without* pointy ears!

"Where do you live, Sylvee?" we inquired. "North of Seattle in Marblemount." "Oh! It all makes sense, Saraina, she's back, she's *back!*"

And so, two weeks after the conference, 'Michael' was old enough to go to his new home. Jeanette traveled north to Marblemount and reunited with her beloved Angel, who returned as an adorable Australian Shepherd/Border Collie mix with a heart-shaped marking on his hip. Jeanette named the playful pup Michael after the Archangel; they connected effortlessly, as did the newcomer with her older dog, Toshi.

Boots

One morning I came home to find a frantic message from Jody. Her usual calm demeanor had given way to panic and tears because Boots, her indoor cat, had gone outdoors unnoticed. To make matters worse, he'd made his way under her car and hid above the wheel well, a discovery she made as she drove off to work in the morning. The loud meow and sudden thud sent her into a whirlwind of emotions as she watched Boots hit the pavement and race off down the street.

Hearing her distressed message, I called immediately. She was deeply concerned that Boots might be hurt or disoriented as he'd never been outside before.

I did my best to calm her (and myself) so I could focus intuitively on Boots. He responded right away and assured me he was not injured, simply hiding; the street noise and people walking by had him lodged in a nearby hedge. He confirmed he would come home once the noise stopped. I estimated his return to be between 1:30 and 2:00 am.

I advised her to put his favorite blanket or bed on the porch along with food and water, as I imagined he would be cold and hungry from his ordeal. I also encouraged her to visualize an energetic connection between her heart and Boots' to help lead him home with her love. All this she did.

I checked my email first thing when I awoke and was over-joyed to find the following message from Jody:

"Man alive, did you nail it when you looked at Boots. At about 1:45 this morning, I heard a cat crying outside. We had put his favorite pillow, food and water out on the porch. Sure enough we opened the door and there sat Boots. He couldn't get in the house fast enough. We picked him up and he just loved on us and purred and purred. He looked a little ragged but walked fine and it didn't seem to bother him when we held him. You were right, he came back after dark and after it was not so noisy and busy. Thank you so much for calling me back as swiftly as you did. I really appreciate your help."

Once again, I thanked the heavens above for our ability to communicate with our beloved pets—beyond language!

Alaskan Medicine Dog

Linda and her husband rescued an American Eskimo dog named Holly. She came with separation anxiety and health issues; although she was bonding with her new owners, she was still fearful of being left behind.

One day Linda found Holly sniffing enthusiastically in her bedroom closet; she walked over and found it was her therapeutic oils in cases on the floor that had grabbed Holly's interest. She began aggressively sniffing around the boxes. A light went on for Linda—these oils can be used for anxiety, emotional release, and treating physical ailments. They work equally well for humans or animals!

Linda opened the boxes; Holly put her nose in the top storage level and started pushing them around, sniffing gleefully. She turned away from some, but with others, especially the Frankincense and Hylichryseum, she went crazy. Linda put the cap on the floor, and Holly rolled on it as if she'd found nirvana. Relieved to see her so happy, they put some on her fur since animals can be very sensitive to oils on their skins (you have to dilute them with carrier oil).

After reveling in the aromas, Holly went right to sleep and slept soundly for the first time in her new home. Her keepers now make sure the essences are available to her any time she requests them. Rapidly her behavioral difficulties have faded into the past: her innate wisdom turned her life around.

Hooney

Hooney needed no invitation; he announced his arrival by strolling through the Weber's front door and moving right in. A massive, long-haired black cat, he was neither shy nor hungry when he appeared. The family took to him quickly; he became a loyal "one-family" pet, keeping to himself when friends or extended family ventured by.

After all, he only had so much time in the day for people. Why waste it on those who don't feed him? He was efficient with his energy and quite observant; when grandbaby Paul arrived, he identified him immediately as a new pack member and purred right up. There was a motive to his methods.

Although he seemed aloof, Hooney had a soft spot—the girls noticed he disappeared each day at the same time for several hours. No one knew where he went, but Gigi was curious enough to find out; like a secret agent, she hid on the porch prior to his departure—she would follow him like a sleuth and discover his secret.

Noon came and like clock-work, Hooney left. Crouched below the wall, our silent spy watched him exit the yard. It didn't take too much detective work to learn his destination; it was the retirement home across the street! He sauntered over to a smattering of seniors enjoying their lunch on the lawn;

methodically he greeted each one in turn, reveling in praise and strokes. His visit was a high point in the day for all.

Did Hooney know that seniors benefit from petting animals? It lowers blood pressure, lifts depression, boosts self-esteem and the immune system. Who could have guessed; Hooney was a self-appointed service cat!

Nallie and Peppy

Nallie, a gentle woman in her 70s, was beginning to lose her hearing. Hearing loss happens so gradually, one might not know they're missing the telephone or door bell. Even more important things like timers or alarm clocks go unnoticed until you get overdone cookies a few too many times.

Peppy, her all-white poodle, was smarter than most people, Nallie would say. Her friend Liz witnessed some proof of this while visiting one afternoon. When the phone rang, she moved to answer it once she realized Nallie couldn't hear it.

But Peppy beat her to it; he ran to the phone, tipped it off the receiver, barked "Hello" into the mouth piece, than ran to fetch Nallie. She strolled over to the phone lying on the rug, thanked Peppy, engaged in a short conversation and returned to visit with Liz.

A few minutes later, the phone rang again. Like lightening, Peppy was on it—you could see the pride he took in being of service. Everyone who called knew his "Hello bark" and the routine that followed. The two were brilliant partners—friends for life and jolly good companions!

Tootsie

A Seal Point Siamese kitten arrived as a birthday present for 8-year-old Debbie. Debbie decided to name her Tootsina, or Tootsie for short; it really wasn't the elegant name she deserved, but her parents honored Debbie's choice since it was her kitty.

Tootsie was strikingly beautiful, with electric blue eyes and fantastic markings; the three sisters adored her and she adored them back! As Tootsie grew, she developed quite a personality. She completely resisted change. The father of this happy home liked to shift things around for variety—the cat scolded him every time a chair moved. It really put her out to see the furniture in different spots. This didn't stop him, so Tootsie meowed a lot.

Debbie's mother and father both worked. The older sisters, Mary and Vickie, watched Debbie after school, and Tootsie watched the big sisters!

It all started when Vickie brought a boyfriend home—the cat confronted him at the door, arching and hissing; it was meticulously apparent she didn't approve of his company. As they made their way past her toward the family room, Tootsie launched an assault from the couch, landing on his back; the frightened beau shrieked in terror while she hung from his shirt. That took the romance out of this visit.

Next, Mary brought a date home on the weekend; Tootsie could care less. This created banter; one boy was a better catch than the other—even the cat could tell. Rivalry ensued until they realized the cat only attacked when the parents weren't home. Gentlemen callers were welcome evenings and weekends, but the chaperone cat would not allow them to be unattended in the house.

The folks were much more amused by this than the sisters—little Debbie didn't care until years later when she brought her sweetheart home from college. It all came back to her—the attacking cat and panicked suitors.

Sure enough, the two were stretched out on the couch watching a movie when Tootsie pounced on his chest. Don't move, she warned the unsuspecting boyfriend; she's quite possessive. The now senior Siamese crept up and sniffed his face (very scary) then settled down on him, investigating thoughtfully. He looked nervous, perhaps a bit pale.

Finally, our feline guardian seemed reasonably content as she licked his arm. Both sighed with relief, then, without provocation, she chomped him on the wrist and took off.... she just couldn't resist giving this little warning: I'm still watching!

Sam and the Land

Mike and Annette were building their first home. Their excitement was growing as the builders laid the foundation and it began to look real. Standing on the property, visualizing how wonderful it was going to be, they were visited by a highly personable brown bear of a dog. He seemed to come out of nowhere; this gentle giant wagged on up to their family, said "Hello," and then went about surveying the property as though he was on a mission.

Months passed, the workers put on the finishing touches, and at last it was time to move in—trucks arrived, boxed were unloaded, and at the end of a very long day the family was finally home! Come the next morning, Annette opened the door to find the big brown dog sitting on the porch. He seemed to believe he belonged here, she remembers, so we adopted him and named him Sam.

Sam's return appearance was a mystery; where had he been while the house was being built and how did he arrive right on cue? Many questions were left unanswered, but his gratitude was evident. He became the loyal guardian of the new 11-month-old baby girl. Everywhere she went he followed. He slept with her and played with her, devoted in everyway—he was an angel in disguise and a parent's best friend.

Now that's a clever Shepard!

Shep and Snowball

In 1931, under the weight of the Depression, Lori and her parents moved to the Mojave Desert; their rustic homestead sat at the end of an isolated road with no electricity or running water. Her playground was canyons, mountains and mesas where singing sand dunes, volcanic cinder cones and carpets of wildflowers flourished.

Shep and Snowball were her loyal companions; Shep was a handsome, long-haired Shepard, regal and brave, and Snowball was an all-white Spitz with *attitude*. The two couldn't have been closer or more opposite.

Although stunning, the Mojave is another world—poisonous creatures crouch in shadows and squiggle under rocks in blistering heat. With no shoes till fall, Lori ran barefoot on the trail; hot sand squished under her thick-soled feet. Shep panted alongside; head up, scouting the way, he paused abruptly, ears pricking, then cut sharply across her path—pressing her legs till she stopped. "What's the matter boy?" she whispered. The furry barricade locked eyes with hers—his silent message: DANGER! DO NOT MOVE! Lori held her breath scanning the terrain—then, she heard it too—the faint rustle of a Rattlesnake poised to strike on the path ahead.

Without skipping a beat, they veered off and headed another direction, leaving the rattler alone in the dust. This is the way of the desert; one must always be present and alert. Her faithful protector pranced ahead, eager for adventure now that the coast was clear. Lori ran alongside, praising his keen senses.

After a long day of play, slanting rays signaled them to journey home. The inhabitants of this harsh ecosystem are nocturnal—they spring forth at dusk; the dangers of night quickly out number you.

Walking back, the crunching of hard rubber wheels over gravel drew her attention to the horizon. There in fading light, she saw father's truck kicking up dust on the rutted red road. She pranced down the hill to greet him, waving her arms, but he wasn't waving back. The dirt was too dense against his gritty windshield; he did not see his running child nor did he slow down as she expected.

Shep sprang to action, clamping his mouth firmly around her forearm, pulling her to a halt as the truck sped by, barely missing her. Lori realized father hadn't seen her at all—she would have been hit if not for Shep's insight and bravery. This garnered more strokes and praise! What an amazing watchdog he was—wise, gentle and knowing—a parent's dream!

Indeed, Shep had a busy life protecting his family; even Snowball counted on him because he was a scrapper with battle scars across his right eye and ear. He never learned to walk away. The worst fight was a coyote—it could've been the end of Snowball but "big brother" charged in, convincing his wily opponent to LEAVE and never return!

It wasn't that Snowball lacked intelligence; he was quite smart, just cocky. He knew things, like how to open the screen door and go in—a skill which proved most useful this fateful day.

Lori and mother were sitting at the table when—BAM—the door flew open, Snowball right behind it. Barking with fury, he looked at the two, then hurriedly raced out—they hadn't time to react when he rushed in again, barking, bouncing off the furniture. He was saying, "FOLLOW ME, FOLLOW ME"!

They jumped to their feet just as he returned a third time and they were off! Snowball trotted as fast as he could, looking back, making sure they were still "in tow"—up, up they went, around the steep butte for over a mile. Lori began worrying and wondering what happened to Shep—the two never parted, he must be injured or worse—she wrenched the unbearable thought out of her mind and focused on ascending in the scorching heat.

Suddenly they saw Shep up ahead motionless on the ground; racing toward him, she strained to see if he was breathing just as his head came up. He was caught in a trap. Shep's gentle face showed great relief as the three arrived—rushing to his side, they soothed and assured him; his leg was injured but not broken. He would be alright!

As they loosened the iron jaws, Snowball pranced frantically, absorbed in the rescue to the point where he neglected his own footing and stepped in a nearby trap. Unlike his cool-tempered elder, he went into full-blown panic—yelping and flailing, forcing them to free him first lest he injure himself further.

Shep sighed audibly, but his eyes still shone with gratitude. His little buddy saved his life; returning with help before larger animals or poisonous creatures found him, a debt of gratitude finally paid.

They released Snowball while Shep waited patiently ... then, he too was finally freed. Snowball could be carried, but Shep was too large, so carefully they limped down the steep hill together.

Back at the cabin, the two were bandaged, fed and tucked in bed. The "brothers" were snoozing side by side, safe and together as they ever shall be.

About the Author

Since 1990, Saraina Hancock has maintained a private practice as a vocational counselor and spiritual mentor in the Pacific Northwest. She specializes in life path and career development. Additionally, she has worked as a vocational rehabilitation consultant for a private company and a vocational counselor and instructor at a community college during the past 12 years.

She has presented workshops and lectures for a wide variety of organizations, including the National Organization for Women's Employment (N.O.W.E.), Work Source, Pathways for Women, YWCA, Shoreline Community College, the Women of Wisdom Foundation and her own company, Para-Dynamics. Her focus is on assisting people of all ages and backgrounds to find "right livelihood"—a vocation that is prosperous, sustainable and meaningful.

In every session, Saraina moves seamlessly between the metaphysical and practical realms, using humor and compassion to increase the level of enjoyment throughout the process of healing and self-discovery.

She believes that a well-balanced approach includes the use of both sides of the mind—left brain for intellectual awareness applied with technical knowledge and the right brain for intuitive wisdom and insights from the field of collective consciousness. This dynamic combination provides deep, long-lasting solutions and inspiration for the evolution of our soul.

She has completed the Clairvoyant Program at the CDM Psychic Institute and holds a Bachelor's and Master's Degree in Psychology from Antioch University in Seattle.

Aside from her professional life, Saraina is an avid animal lover, committed to advocating for and supporting both domestic and wild animals. Please visit her websites for more information: www.phenomenalpets.com and www.stateofmindcounseling.net.

References

1. Abram, D.1997. The Spell of the Sensuous: Perception and language in a more-than-human world. Vintage Books, a division of Random House, Inc. New York, New York.

2. Dyer, W. 2005. The Power of Intention on PBS [Audiobook] Hay House Audio; 140190355X

3. Byrne, R., Harrington, P., Heriot, D. 2006. The Secret [DVD]. Prime Time Productions. Australia.

4. McTaggart, L. 2001. The Field: The quest for the secret force of the universe. HarperCollins, New York, New York.

5. McTaggart, L. 2001. The Field: The quest for the secret force of the universe. HarperCollins, New York, New York.

6. Capra, F. 1996. The Web of Life: A new scientific understanding of living systems. Anchor Books, A division of Random House, Inc. New York, New York.

7. Boone, J. 1976. Kinship with all life. Harper & Row Publishers, San Francisco, California.

8. Damrosch, B. 1888. The Garden Primer. Workman Publishing Company, New York, New York.

9. Capra, F. 1988. Turning Point: Science, society and rising culture. Fontana Paperbacks. London, England

10. Carson, D. & Sams, J. 1988. Medicine Cards: The discovery of power through the ways of animals. Bear & Company. Santa Fe, New Mexico.

11. Arntz, W., Chasse, B., Hoffman, M. (2005). *What the BLEEP do we (K)now?!* [Motion picture] Lord of the Wind Films, LLC. 20th Century Fox.

12. Blum, R. 1982. The Book of Runes. St. Martin's Press, New York, New York.

13. Dark Night of the Soul. Wikipedia: The Free Encyclopedia Retrieved 2006 from:
    http://en.wikipedia.org/wiki/Dark_Night_of_the_Soul

14. Dyer, W. 2005. The Power of Intention on PBS [Audiobook] Hay House Audio; 140190355X

15. Arntz, W., Chasse, B., Hoffman, M. (2005). What the [BLEEP] do we {K}now?!. [Motion picture] Lord of the Wind Films, LLC. 20th Century Fox

16. Alder, N. 1979. Einstein's Universe. Penguin Books, New York, New York.

978-0-595-44261-4
0-595-44261-7

www.ingramcontent.com/pod-product-compliance
Lightning Source LLC
Chambersburg PA
CBHW022254290526
45785CB00015B/1000